WHOEVER BROUGHT ME HERE
WILL HAVE TO TAKE ME HOME

Called 'Jelaluddin Balkhi' by the Persians and Afghans, Rumi was born on September 30, 1207, in Balkh, Afghanistan, then a part of the Persian Empire. Between 1215 and 1220, he and his family fled the threat of the invading Mongols and emigrated to Konya, Turkey; it was sometime after this that he became known as 'Rumi' meaning 'from Roman Anatolia'. His father, Bahauddin Walad, was a theologian and a mystic, and after his death Rumi took over the role of sheikh in the dervish learning community in Konya. Rumi pursued the life of an orthodox religious scholar until 1244 when he encountered the wandering dervish, Shams of Tabriz. After an exchange of religious ideas Shams and Rumi became inseparable friends, transported into a world of pure, mystical, conversation. This intense relationship left Rumi's students feeling neglected, and, feeling the ill-will, Shams disappeared. After news of Shams came from Damascus, Rumi's son was sent to bring him back, and the mystical conversation, or *sohbet*, began again. After Shams' second disappearance (he was probably murdered), and a period spent searching for his lost friend, Rumi came to the conclusion that Shams was now a part of him. Further concluding that when he wrote poetry it was Shams writing through him, he called his huge collection of odes and quatrains *The Works of Shams of Tabriz*. Following Shams' death Rumi had two other mystical companions, firstly Saladin Zarkub, a goldsmith, and then, after Saladin's death, Husam Chelebi, Rumi's scribe and student. It was Husam that Rumi declared the source of his vast six-volume masterwork *Mathnawi*. After twelve years of work on this masterpiece Rumi died on December 17, 1273.

Coleman Barks is Emeritus Professor of English at the University of Georgia in Athens, Georgia. Since 1984 he has, in collaboration with various Persian scholars, worked on translations of Rumi's poetry. Many consider that this compendium set, originally published as *The Essential Rumi*, has made the 13th century mystic the most-read poet in the United States.

Whoever Brought Me Here
Will Have to Take Me Home

RUMI

Translated by COLEMAN BARKS
with JOHN MOYNE

ARKANA
PENGUIN BOOKS

for the compassionate heart within the mind, the light within the body,

ARKANA

Published by the Penguin Group
27 Wrights Lane, London W8 5TZ, England
Penguin Putnam Inc., 375 Hudson Street, New York, New York 10014, USA
Penguin Books Australia Ltd, Ringwood, Victoria, Australia
Penguin Books Canada Ltd, 10 Alcorn Avenue, Toronto, Ontario, Canada M4V 3B2
Penguin Books (NZ) Ltd, 182–190 Wairau Road, Auckland 10, New Zealand

Penguin Books Ltd, Registered Offices: Harmondsworth, Middlesex, England

These translations first published in the USA in *The Essential Rumi* by HarperCollins 1995
Published by Arkana 1998
10 9 8 7 6 5 4 3 2 1

Set in 10/12.5 pt PostScript Monotype Bembo
Typeset by Rowland Phototypesetting Ltd, Bury St Edmunds, Suffolk
Made and printed in Great Britain by Clays Ltd, St Ives plc

Contents

8. *Being a Lover: The Sunrise Ruby*

On Rumi

Persians and Afghanis call Rumi 'Jelaluddin Balkhi'. He was born September 30, 1207, in Balkh, Afghanistan, which was then part of the Persian empire. The name *Rumi* means 'from Roman Anatolia.' He was not known by that name, of course, until after his family, fleeing the threat of the invading Mongol armies, emigrated to Konya, Turkey, sometime between 1215 and 1220. His father, Bahauddin Walad, was a theologian and jurist and a mystic of uncertain lineage. Bahauddin Walad's *Maarif*, a collection of notes, diarylike remarks, sermons, and strange accounts of visionary experiences, has shocked most of the conventional scholars who have tried to understand them. He shows a startlingly sensual freedom in stating his union with God. Rumi was instructed in his father's secret inner life by a former student of his father, Burhanuddin Mahaqqiq. Burhan and Rumi also studied Sanai and Attar. At his father's death Rumi took over the position of sheikh in the dervish learning community in Konya. His life seems to have been a fairly normal one for a religious scholar – teaching, meditating, helping the poor – until in the late fall of 1244 when he met a stranger who put a question to him. That stranger was the wandering dervish, Shams of Tabriz, who had traveled throughout the Middle East searching and praying for someone who could 'endure my company.' A voice came, 'What will you give in return?' 'My head!' 'The one you seek is Jelaluddin of Konya.'

The question Shams spoke made the learned professor faint to the ground. We cannot be entirely certain of the question, but according to the most reliable account Shams asked who was greater, Muhammad or Bestami, for Bestami had said, 'How great is my glory,' whereas Muhammad had acknowledged in his prayer to God, 'We do not know You as we should.'

Rumi heard the depth out of which the question came and fell to the ground. He was finally able to answer that Muhammad was greater, because Bestami had taken one gulp of the divine and stopped there, whereas for Muhammad the way was always unfolding. There are various versions of this encounter, but whatever the facts, Shams and Rumi became inseparable. Their Friendship is one of the mysteries. They spent months together without any human needs, transported into a region of pure conversation. This ecstatic connection caused difficulties in the religious community. Rumi's students felt neglected. Sensing the trouble, Shams disappeared as suddenly as he had appeared. Annemarie Schimmel, a scholar immersed for forty years in the works of Rumi, thinks that it was at this first disappearance that Rumi began the transformation into a mystical artist. 'He turned into a poet, began to listen to music, and sang, whirling around, hour after hour.'

Word came that Shams was in Damascus. Rumi sent his son, Sultan Velad, to Syria to bring his Friend back to Konya. When Rumi and Shams met for the second time, they fell at each other's feet, so that 'no one knew who was lover and who the beloved.' Shams stayed in Rumi's home and was married to a young girl who had been brought up in the family. Again the long mystical conversation (*sohbet*) began, and again the jealousies grew.

On the night of December 5, 1248, as Rumi and Shams were talking, Shams was called to the back door. He went out, never to be seen again. Most likely, he was murdered with the connivance of Rumi's son, Allaedin; if so, Shams indeed gave his head for the privilege of mystical Friendship.

The mystery of the Friend's absence covered Rumi's world. He himself went out searching for Shams and journeyed again to Damascus. It was there that he realized,

Why should I seek? I am the same as
he. His essence speaks through me.
I have been looking for myself!

The union became complete. There was full *fana*, annihilation in the Friend. Shams was writing the poems. Rumi called the huge collection of his odes and quatrains *The Works of Shams of Tabriz*.

After Shams's death and Rumi's merging with him, another companion was found, Saladin Zarkub, the goldsmith. Saladin became the Friend to whom Rumi addressed his poems, not so fierily as to Shams, but with quiet tenderness. When Saladin died, Husam Chelebi, Rumi's scribe and favorite student, assumed this role. Rumi claimed that Husam was the source, the one who understood the vast, secret order of the *Mathnawi*, that great work that shifts so fantastically from theory to folklore to jokes to ecstatic poetry. For the last twelve years of his life, Rumi dictated the six volumes of this masterwork to Husam. He died on December 17, 1273.

A Note on the Organization

The design of this series of Rumi books is meant to confuse scholars who would divide Rumi's poetry into the accepted categories: the quatrains (*rubaiyat*) and odes (*ghazals*) of the *Divan*, the six books of the *Mathnawi*, the discourses, the letters, and the almost unknown *Six Sermons*. The mind wants categories, but Rumi's creativity was a continuous fountaining from beyond forms and the mind, or as the sufis say, from a mind within the mind, the *qalb*, which is a great compassionate generosity.

The eight divisions here, and the twenty-seven in the series, are faint and playful palimpsests spread over Rumi's imagination. Poems easily splash over, slide from one overlay to another. The theme of these eight sections might be said to be the ecstasy of the lover's waking. The unity behind, *La'illaha il'Allahu* ('there's no reality but God; there is only God'), is the one substance the other subheadings float within at various depths. If one actually selected an 'essential' Rumi, it would be the *zikr*, the remembering that everything is God. Likewise, the titles of the poems are whimsical. Rumi's individual poems in Persian have no titles. His collection of quatrains and odes is called *The Works of Shams of Tabriz* (*Divani Shamsi Tabriz*). The six books of poetry he dictated to his scribe, Husam Chelebi, are simply titled *Spiritual Couplets* (*Mathnawi*), or sometimes he refers to them as *The Book of Husam*. The wonderfully goofy title of the discourses, *In It What's in It* (*Fihi Ma Fihi*), may mean 'what's in the *Mathnawi* is in this too,' or it may be the kind of hands-thrown-up gesture it sounds like.

All of which makes the point that these poems are not monumental in the Western sense of memorializing moments; they are not discrete entities but a fluid, continuously self-revising, self-interrupting *medium*. They are not so much *about* anything as spoken from *within* something.

Call it enlightenment, ecstatic love, spirit, soul, truth, the ocean of *ilm* (divine luminous wisdom), or the covenant of *alast* (the original agreement with God). Names do not matter. Some resonance of ocean resides in everyone. Rumi's poetry can be felt as a salt breeze from that, traveling inland.

These poems were created, not in packets and batches of art, but as part of a constant, practical, and mysterious discourse Rumi was having with a dervish learning community. The focus changed from stern to ecstatic, from everyday to esoteric, as the needs of the group arose. Poetry and music and movement were parts of that communal and secretly individual work of opening hearts and exploring the mystery of union with the divine. The form of this collection means to honor the variety and simultaneity of that mystical union.

Most of the facts, dates, and chew-toys for the intellect are stashed in the Notes.

Rumi puts a prose prayer at the beginning of each book of the *Mathnawi*. Here's the blessing he gives before Book IV.

Praise to Early-Waking Grievers
In the name of God the Most Merciful, and the Most Compassionate.

This is the fourth journey toward home, toward where the great advantages are waiting for us. Reading it, mystics will feel very happy, as a meadow feels when it hears thunder, the good news of rain coming, as tired eyes look forward to sleeping. Joy for the spirit, health for the body. In here is what genuine devotion wants, refreshment, sweet fruit ripe enough for the pickiest picker, medicine, detailed directions on how to get to the Friend. All praise to God. Here is the way to renew connection with your soul, and rest from difficulties. The study of this book will be painful to those who feel separate from God. It will make the others grateful. In the hold of this ship is a cargo not found in the attractiveness of young women. Here is a reward for lovers of God. A full moon and an inheritance you thought you had lost are now returned to you. More hope for the hopeful, lucky finds for foragers, wonderful things thought of to do. Anticipation after depression, expanding after contraction. The sun comes out, and that light is what we give, in this book, to our spiritual descendants. Our gratitude to God holds them to us, and brings more besides. As the Andalusian poet, Adi al-Riga, says,

I was sleeping, and being comforted
by a cool breeze, when suddenly a gray dove
from a thicket sang and sobbed with longing,
and reminded me of my own passion.

I had been away from my own soul so long,
so late-sleeping, but that dove's crying
woke me and made me cry. *Praise*
to all early-waking grievers!

Some go first, and others come long afterward. God blesses both and all in the
line, and replaces what has been consumed, and provides for those who work
the soil of helpfulness, and blesses Muhammad and Jesus and every other
messenger and prophet. Amen, and may the Lord of all created beings bless
you.

1. The Tavern:

Whoever Brought Me Here Will Have to Take Me Home

ON THE TAVERN

In the tavern are many wines – the wine of delight in color and form and taste, the wine of the intellect's agility, the fine port of stories, and the cabernet of soul singing. Being human means entering this place where entrancing varieties of desire are served. The grapeskin of ego breaks and a pouring begins. Fermentation is one of the oldest symbols of human transformation. When grapes combine their juice and are closed up together for a time in a dark place, the results are spectacular. This is what lets two drunks meet so that they don't know who is who. Pronouns no longer apply in the tavern's mud-world of excited confusion and half-articulated wantings.

But after some time in the tavern, a point comes, a memory of elsewhere, a longing for the source, and the drunks must set off from the tavern and begin the return. The Qur'an says, 'We are all returning.' The tavern is a kind of glorious hell that human beings enjoy and suffer and then push off from in their search for truth. The tavern is a dangerous region where sometimes disguises are necessary, but never hide your heart, Rumi urges. Keep open there. A breaking apart, a crying out into the street, begins in the tavern, and the human soul turns to find its way home.

It's 4 A.M. Nasruddin leaves the tavern and walks the town aimlessly. A policeman stops him. 'Why are you out wandering the streets in the middle of the night?' 'Sir,' replies Nasruddin, 'if I knew the answer to that question, I would have been home hours ago!'

Who Says Words with My Mouth?

All day I think about it, then at night I say it.
Where did I come from, and what am I supposed to be doing?
I have no idea.
My soul is from elsewhere, I'm sure of that,
and I intend to end up there.

This drunkenness began in some other tavern.
When I get back around to that place,
I'll be completely sober. Meanwhile,
I'm like a bird from another continent, sitting in this aviary.
The day is coming when I fly off,
but who is it now in my ear who hears my voice?
Who says words with my mouth?

Who looks out with my eyes? What is the soul?
I cannot stop asking.
If I could taste one sip of an answer,
I could break out of this prison for drunks.
I didn't come here of my own accord, and I can't leave that way.
Whoever brought me here will have to take me home.

This poetry. I never know what I'm going to say.
I don't plan it.
When I'm outside the saying of it,
I get very quiet and rarely speak at all.

*   *   *   *

We have a huge barrel of wine, but no cups.
That's fine with us. Every morning
we glow and in the evening we glow again.

They say there's no future for us. They're right.
Which is fine with us.

* * * *

A Community of the Spirit

There is a community of the spirit.
Join it, and feel the delight
of walking in the noisy street,
and *being* the noise.

Drink *all* your passion,
and be a disgrace.

Close both eyes
to see with the other eye.

Open your hands,
if you want to be held.

Sit down in this circle.

Quit acting like a wolf, and feel
the shepherd's love filling you.

At night, your beloved wanders.
Don't accept consolations.

Close your mouth against food.
Taste the lover's mouth in yours.

You moan, 'She left me.' 'He left me.'
Twenty more will come.

Be empty of worrying.
Think of who created thought!

Why do you stay in prison
when the door is so wide open?

Move outside the tangle of fear-thinking.
Live in silence.

Flow down and down in always
widening rings of being.

*   *   *   *

There's a strange frenzy in my head,
of birds flying,
each particle circulating on its own.
Is the one I love *everywhere*?

*   *   *   *

Drunks fear the police,
but the police are drunk too.

People in this town love them both
like different chess pieces.

*   *   *   *

A Children's Game

Listen to the poet Sanai,
who lived secluded: 'Don't wander out on the road
in your ecstasy. Sleep in the tavern.'

When a drunk strays out to the street,
children make fun of him.

                              He falls down in the mud.
He takes any and every road.

                              The children follow,
not knowing the taste of wine, or how
his drunkenness feels. All people on the planet
are children, except for a very few.
No one is grown up except those free of desire.

God said,

          'The world is a play, a children's game,
and you are the children.'

                              God speaks the truth.
If you haven't left the child's play,
how can you be an adult?

                              Without purity of spirit,
if you're still in the middle of lust and greed
and other wantings, you're like children
playing at sexual intercourse.

                              They wrestle
and rub together, but it's not sex!

The same with the fightings of mankind.
It's a squabble with play-swords.
No purpose, totally futile.

Like kids on hobby horses, soldiers claim to be riding
Boraq, Muhammad's night-horse, or Duldul, his mule.

Your actions mean nothing, the sex and war that you do.
You're holding part of your pants and prancing around,
Dun-da-dun, dun-da-dun.

Don't wait till you die to see this.
Recognize that your imagination and your thinking
and your sense perception are reed canes
that children cut and pretend are horsies.

The knowing of mystic lovers is different.
The empirical, sensory, sciences
are like a donkey loaded with books,
or like the makeup woman's makeup.
                                        It washes off.
But if you lift the baggage rightly, it will give joy.
Don't carry your knowledge-load for some selfish reason.
Deny your desires and willfulness,
and a real mount may appear under you.

Don't be satisfied with the *name* of HU,
with just words about it.

Experience *that breathing*.
From books and words come fantasy,
and sometimes, from fantasy comes union.

*   *   *   *

Gone, inner and outer,
no moon, nor ground or sky.

Don't hand me another glass of wine.
Pour it in my mouth.
I've lost the way to my mouth.

* * * *

The wine we really drink is our own blood.
Our bodies ferment in these barrels.
We give everything for a glass of this.
We give our minds for a sip.

* * * *

The Many Wines

God has given us a dark wine so potent that,
drinking it, we leave the two worlds.

God has put into the form of hashish a power
to deliver the taster from self-consciousness.

God has made sleep so
that it erases every thought.

God made Majnun love Layla so much that
just her dog would cause confusion in him.

There are thousands of wines
that can take over our minds.

Don't think all ecstasies
are the same!

Jesus was lost in his love for God.
His donkey was drunk with barley.

Drink from the presence of saints,
not from those other jars.

Every object, every being,
is a jar full of delight.

Be a connoisseur,
and taste with caution.

Any wine will get you high.
Judge like a king, and choose the purest,

the ones unadulterated with fear,
or some urgency about 'what's needed.'

Drink the wine that moves you
as a camel moves when it's been untied,
and is just ambling about.

Special Plates

Notice how each particle moves.
Notice how everyone has just arrived here
                    from a journey.
Notice how each wants a different food.
Notice how the stars vanish as the sun comes up,
                    and how all streams stream toward the ocean.

Look at the chefs preparing special plates
                    for everyone, according to what they need.
Look at this cup that can hold the ocean.
Look at those who see the face.
Look through Shams' eyes
                    into the water that is
                    entirely jewels.

Burnt Kabob

Last year, I admired wines. This,
I'm wandering inside the red world.

Last year, I gazed at the fire.
This year I'm burnt kabob.

Thirst drove me down to the water
where I drank the moon's reflection.

Now I am a lion staring up totally
lost in love with the thing itself.

Don't ask questions about longing.
Look in my face.

Soul drunk, body ruined, these two
sit helpless in a wrecked wagon.
Neither knows how to fix it.

And my heart, I'd say it was more
like a donkey sunk in a mudhole,
struggling and miring deeper.

But listen to me: for one moment,
quit being sad. Hear blessings
dropping their blossoms
around you. God.

The New Rule

It's the old rule that drunks have to argue
and get into fights.
The lover is just as bad. He falls into a hole.
But down in that hole he finds something shining,
worth more than any amount of money or power.

Last night the moon came dropping its clothes in the street.
I took it as a sign to start singing,
falling up into the bowl of sky.
The bowl breaks. Everywhere is falling everywhere.
Nothing else to do.

Here's the new rule: break the wineglass,
and fall toward the glassblower's breath.

*   *   *   *

This that is tormented and very tired,
tortured with restraints like a madman,
this heart.
　　　　　Still you keep breaking the shell
to get the taste of its kernel!

2. Bewilderment:

I Have Five Things to Say

ON BEWILDERMENT

At the verge of full *fana* (annihilation in God) there seems to be a region
of sweet confusion, the sense of being in many places at once saying
multiple sentences. A hazy melting, fragile and nearly blank. Profound
ignorance within which conventional, calm behavior seems *insane!*

Rumi's poems are not well-trimmed, Persian miniature gardens.
They are more like, as scholar Annemarie Schimmel says, the paintings
in the Turkoman style – full of abrupt movement, odd flowers and
bushes, demons and talking animals.

I Have Five Things to Say

The wakened lover speaks directly to the beloved,
'You are the sky my spirit circles in,
the love inside love, the resurrection-place.

Let this window be your ear.
I have lost consciousness many times
with longing for your listening silence,
and your life-quickening smile.

You give attention to the smallest matters,
my suspicious doubts, and to the greatest.

You know my coins are counterfeit,
but you accept them anyway,
my impudence and my pretending!

I have five things to say,
five fingers to give
into your grace.

First, when I was apart from you,
        this world did not exist,
            nor any other.

Second, whatever I was looking for
        was always you.

Third, why did I ever learn to count to three?

Fourth, my cornfield is burning!

Fifth, this finger stands for Rabia,
        and this is for someone else.
            Is there a difference?

Are these words or tears?
Is weeping speech?
What shall I do, my love?'

So he speaks, and everyone around
begins to cry with him, laughing crazily,
moaning in the spreading union
of lover and beloved.

This is the true religion. All others
are thrown-away bandages beside it.

This is the *sema* of slavery and mastery
dancing together. This is not-being.

Neither words, nor any natural fact
can express this.

I know these dancers.
Day and night I sing their songs
in this phenomenal cage.

My soul, don't try to answer now!
Find a friend, and hide.

But what can stay hidden?
Love's secret is always lifting its head
out from under the covers,
'Here I am!'

Acts of Helplessness

Here are the miracle-signs you want: that
you cry through the night and get up at dawn, asking,
that in the absence of what you ask for your day gets dark,
your neck thin as a spindle, that what you give away
is all you own, that you sacrifice belongings,
sleep, health, your head, that you often
sit down in a fire like aloes wood, and often go out
to meet a blade like a battered helmet.

When acts of helplessness become habitual,
those are the *signs*.

But you run back and forth listening for unusual events,
peering into the faces of travelers.

'Why are you looking at me like a madman?'
I have lost a friend. Please forgive me.

Searching like that does not fail.
There will come a rider who holds you close.
You faint and gibber. The uninitiated say, 'He's faking.'
How could they know?
Water washes over a beached fish, the water
of those signs I just mentioned.

Excuse my wandering.
How can one be orderly with this?
It's like counting leaves in a garden,
along with the song-notes of partridges,
and crows.
            Sometimes organization
and computation become absurd.

Saladin's Begging Bowl

Of these two thousand 'I' and 'We' people,
which am I?

Don't try to keep me from asking!
Listen, when I'm this out of control!
But don't put anything breakable in my way!

There is an original inside me.
What's here is a mirror for that, for you.

If you are joyful, I am.
If you grieve, or if you're bitter, or graceful,
I take on those qualities.

Like the shadow of a cypress tree in the meadow,
like the shadow of a rose, I live
close to the rose.

If I separated myself from you,
I would turn entirely thorn.

Every second, I drink another cup of my own blood-wine.
Every instant, I break an empty cup against your door.

I reach out, wanting you to tear me open.

Saladin's generosity lights a candle in my chest.
Who *am* I then?
                    His empty begging bowl.

*   *   *   *

Late, by myself, in the boat of myself,
no light and no land anywhere,
cloudcover thick. I try to stay
just above the surface, yet I'm already under
and living within the ocean.

*   *   *   *

Does sunset sometimes look like the sun's coming up?
Do you know what a faithful love is like?

You're crying. You say you've burned yourself.
But can you think of anyone who's not
hazy with smoke?

*   *   *   *

Be Melting Snow

Totally conscious, and apropos of nothing, you come to see me.
Is someone here? I ask.
The moon. The full moon is inside your house.

My friends and I go running out into the street.
I'm in here, comes a voice from the house, but we aren't listening.
We're looking up at the sky.
My pet nightingale sobs like a drunk in the garden.
Ringdoves scatter with small cries, *Where, Where*.
It's midnight. The whole neighborhood is up and out
in the street thinking, *The cat burglar has come back.*
The actual thief is there too, saying out loud,
Yes, the cat burglar is somewhere in this crowd.
No one pays attention.

Lo, I am with you always means when you look for God,
God is in the look of your eyes,
in the thought of looking, nearer to you than your self,
or things that have happened to you.
There's no need to go outside.

Be melting snow.
Wash yourself of yourself.

A white flower grows in the quietness.
Let your tongue become that flower.

The Fragile Vial

I need a mouth as wide as the sky
to say the nature of a True Person, language
as large as longing.

The fragile vial inside me often breaks.
No wonder I go mad and disappear for three days
every month with the moon.

For anyone in love with you,
it's always these invisible days.

I've lost the thread of the story I was telling.
My elephant roams his dream of Hindustan again.
Narrative, poetics, destroyed, my body,
a dissolving, a return.

Friend, I've shrunk to a hair trying to say your story.
Would you tell mine?
I've made up so many love stories.
Now I feel fictional.
Tell *me!*
The truth is, you are speaking, not me.
I am Sinai, and you are Moses walking there.
This poetry is an echo of what you say.
A piece of land can't speak, or know anything!
Or if it can, only within limits.

The body is a device to calculate
the astronomy of the spirit.
Look through that astrolabe
and become oceanic.

Why this distracted talk?
It's not my fault I rave.
You did this.
Do you approve of my love-madness?

Say yes.
What language will you say it in, Arabic or Persian,
or what? Once again, I must be tied up.

Bring the curly ropes of your hair.

                              Now I remember the story.

A True Man stares at his old shoes
and sheepskin jacket. Every day he goes up
to his attic to look at his work-shoes and worn-out coat.
This is his wisdom, to remember the original clay
and not get drunk with ego and arrogance.

To visit those shoes and jacket
is praise.

The Absolute works with nothing.
The workshop, the materials
are what does not exist.

Try and be a sheet of paper with nothing on it.
Be a spot of ground where nothing is growing,
where something might be planted,
a seed, possibly, from the Absolute.

Where Are We?

An invisible bird flies over,
but casts a quick shadow.

What is the body? That shadow of a shadow
of your love, that somehow contains
the entire universe.

A man sleeps heavily,
though something blazes in him like the sun,
like a magnificent fringe sewn up under the hem.

He turns under the covers.
Any image is a lie:

    A clear red stone tastes sweet.

    You kiss a beautiful mouth, and a key
    turns in the lock of your fear.

    A spoken sentence sharpens to a fine edge.

    A mother dove looks for her nest,
    asking where, *ku?* Where, *ku?*

Where the lion lies down.
Where any man or woman goes to cry.
Where the sick go when they hope to get well.

Where a wind lifts that helps with winnowing,
and, the same moment, sends a ship on its way.

Where anyone says *Only God Is Real.*
Ya Hu! Where beyond *where.*

A bright weaver's shuttle flashes back and forth,
east–west, *Where-are-we? Ma ku? Maku.*
like the sun saying *Where are we?*
as it weaves with the asking.

*   *   *   *

The Friend comes into my body
looking for the center, unable
to find it, draws a blade,
strikes anywhere.

*   *   *   *

There is a light seed grain inside.
You fill it with yourself, or it dies.

I'm caught in this curling energy! Your hair!
Whoever's calm and sensible is insane!

*   *   *   *

Do you think I know what I'm doing?
That for one breath or half-breath I belong to myself?
As much as a pen knows what it's writing,
or the ball can guess where it's going next.

3. Emptiness and Silence:
The Night Air

ON SILENCE

In Persian poetry the poet often refers to himself or herself by name at the end of a poem as a sort of signature. Rumi's variation on this is to refer instead to Shams (over a thousand poems end this way) or to silence. He gives the poetry to its true authorship, including the emptiness *after* as part of the poem. Five hundred odes conclude with *khamush*, silence. Rumi is less interested in language, more attuned to the sources of it. He keeps asking Husam, 'Who's making this music?' He sometimes gives the wording over to the invisible flute player: 'Let that musician finish this poem.' Words are not important in themselves, but as resonators for a center. Rumi has a whole theory of language based on the reed flute (*ney*). Beneath everything we say, and within each note of the reed flute, lies a nostalgia for the reed bed. Language and music are possible only because we're empty, hollow, and separated from the source. All language is a longing for home. Why is there not a second tonality, he muses, a note in praise of the craftsman's skill, which fashioned the bare cylinder into a *ney*, the intricate human form with its nine holes?

The Reed Flute's Song

Listen to the story told by the reed,
of being separated.

'Since I was cut from the reedbed,
I have made this crying sound.

Anyone apart from someone he loves
understands what I say.

Anyone pulled from a source
longs to go back.

At any gathering I am there,
mingling in the laughing and grieving,

a friend to each, but few
will hear the secrets hidden

within the notes. No ears for that.
Body flowing out of spirit,

spirit up from body: no concealing
that mixing. But it's not given us

to *see* the soul. The reed flute
is fire, not wind. Be that empty.'

Hear the love fire tangled
in the reed notes, as bewilderment

melts into wine. The reed is a friend
to all who want the fabric torn

and drawn away. The reed is hurt
and salve combining. Intimacy

and longing for intimacy, one
song. A disastrous surrender

and a fine love, together. The one
who secretly hears this is senseless.

A tongue has one customer, the ear.
A sugarcane flute has such effect

because it was able to make sugar
in the reedbed. The sound it makes

is for everyone. Days full of wanting,
let them go by without worrying

that they do. Stay where you are
inside such a pure, hollow note.

Every thirst gets satisfied except
that of these fish, the mystics,

who swim a vast ocean of grace
still somehow longing for it!

No one lives in that without
being nourished every day.

But if someone doesn't want to hear
the song of the reed flute,

it's best to cut conversation
short, say good-bye, and leave.

A Thirsty Fish

I don't get tired of you. Don't grow weary
of being compassionate toward me!

All this thirst equipment
must surely be *tired* of me,
the waterjar, the water carrier.

I have a thirsty fish in me
that can never find enough
of what it's thirsty for!

Show me the way to the ocean!
Break these half-measures,
these small containers.

All this fantasy
and grief.

Let my house be drowned in the wave
that rose last night out of the courtyard
hidden in the center of my chest.

Joseph fell like the moon into my well.
The harvest I expected was washed away.
But no matter.

A fire has risen above my tombstone hat.
I don't want learning, or dignity,
or respectability.

I want this music and this dawn
and the warmth of your cheek against mine.

The grief-armies assemble,
but I'm not going with them.

This is how it always is
when I finish a poem.

A great silence overcomes me,
and I wonder why I ever thought
to use language.

Enough Words?

How does a part of the world leave the world?
How can wetness leave water?

Don't try to put out a fire
by throwing on more fire!
Don't wash a wound with blood!

No matter how fast you run,
your shadow more than keeps up.
Sometimes, it's in front!

Only full, overhead sun
diminishes your shadow.

But that shadow has been serving you!
What hurts you, blesses you.
Darkness is your candle.
Your boundaries are your quest.

I can explain this, but it would break
the glass cover on your heart,
and there's no fixing that.

You must have shadow and light source both.
Listen, and lay your head under the tree of awe.

When from that tree, feathers and wings sprout
on you, be quieter than a dove.
Don't open your mouth for even a *cooooooo*.

When a frog slips into the water, the snake
cannot get it. Then the frog climbs back out
and croaks, and the snake moves toward him again.

Even if the frog learned to hiss, still the snake
would hear through the hiss the information
he needed, the frog voice underneath.

But if the frog could be completely silent,
then the snake would go back to sleeping,
and the frog could reach the barley.

The soul lives there in the silent breath.

And that grain of barley is such that,
when you put it in the ground,
it grows.
            Are these enough words,
or shall I squeeze more juice from this?
Who am I, my friend?

This World Which Is Made of Our Love
for Emptiness

Praise to the emptiness that blanks out existence. Existence:
this place made from our love for that emptiness!
Yet somehow comes emptiness,
this existence goes.
Praise to that happening, over and over!

For years I pulled my own existence out of emptiness.
Then one swoop, one swing of the arm,
that work is over.
Free of who I was, free of presence, free of
dangerous fear, hope,
free of mountainous wanting.

The here-and-now mountain is a tiny piece of a piece
of straw
blown off into emptiness.

These words I'm saying so much begin to lose meaning:
existence, emptiness, mountain, straw: words
and what they try to say swept
out the window, down the slant of the roof.

Quietness

Inside this new love, die.
Your way begins on the other side.
Become the sky.
Take an axe to the prison wall.
Escape.
Walk out like someone suddenly born into color.
Do it now.
You're covered with thick cloud.
Slide out the side. Die,
and be quiet. Quietness is the surest sign
that you've died.
Your old life was a frantic running
from silence.

The speechless full moon
comes out now.

Sanai

Someone says, *Sanai is dead.*
No small thing to say.

He was not bits of husk,
or a puddle that freezes overnight,
or a comb that cracks when you use it,
or a pod crushed open on the ground.

He was fine powder in a rough clay dish.
He knew what both worlds were worth:
A grain of barley.

One he slung down, the other up.

The inner soul, that presence of which most know nothing,
about which poets are so ambiguous,
he married that one to the beloved.

His pure gold wine pours on the thick wine dregs.
They mix and rise and separate again
to meet down the road. Dear friend from Marghaz,
who lived in Rayy, in Rum, Kurd from the mountains,
each of us returns home.

Silk must not be compared with striped canvas.

Be quiet and clear now
like the final touchpoints of calligraphy.

Your name has been erased
from the roaring volume of speech.

A Just-Finishing Candle

A candle is made to become entirely flame.
In that annihilating moment
it has no shadow.

It is nothing but a tongue of light
describing a refuge.

Look at this
just-finishing candle stub
as someone who is finally safe
from virtue and vice,

the pride and the shame
we claim from those.

Craftsmanship and Emptiness

I've said before that every craftsman
searches for what's not there
to practice his craft.

A builder looks for the rotten hole
where the roof caved in. A water carrier
picks the empty pot. A carpenter
stops at the house with no door.

Workers rush toward some hint
of emptiness, which they then
start to fill. Their hope, though,
is for emptiness, so don't think
you must avoid it. It contains

what you need!
                    Dear soul, if you were not friends
with the vast nothing inside,
why would you always be casting your net
into it, and waiting so patiently?

This invisible ocean has given you such abundance,
but still you call it 'death,'
that which provides you sustenance and work.

God has allowed some magical reversal to occur,
so that you see the scorpion pit
as an object of desire,
and all the beautiful expanse around it
as dangerous and swarming with snakes.

This is how strange your fear of death
and emptiness is, and how perverse
the attachment to what you want.

Now that you've heard me
on your misapprehensions, dear friend,
listen to Attar's story on the same subject.

He strung the pearls of this
about King Mahmud, how among the spoils
of his Indian campaign there was a Hindu boy,
whom he adopted as a son. He educated
and provided royally for the boy
and later made him vice-regent, seated
on a gold throne beside himself.

One day he found the young man weeping.
'Why are you crying? You're the companion
of an emperor! The entire nation is ranged out
before you like stars that you can command!'

The young man replied, 'I am remembering
my mother and my father, and how they
scared me as a child with threats of you!
"Uh-oh, he's headed for King Mahmud's court!
Nothing could be more hellish!" Where are they now
when they should see me sitting here?'

This incident is about your fear of changing.
You are the Hindu boy. *Mahmud*, which means,
Praise to the End, is the spirit's
poverty, or emptiness.

The mother and father are your attachment
to beliefs and bloodties
and desires and comforting habits.

Don't listen to them!
They seem to protect,
but they imprison.

They are your worst enemies.
They make you afraid
of living in emptiness.

Some day you'll weep tears of delight in that court,
remembering your mistaken parents!

Know that your body nurtures the spirit,
helps it grow, and then gives it wrong advice.

The body becomes, eventually, like a vest
of chainmail in peaceful years,
too hot in summer and too cold in winter.

But the body's desires, in another way, are like
an unpredictable associate, whom you must be
patient with. And that companion is helpful,
because patience expands your capacity
to love and feel peace.

The patience of a rose close to a thorn
keeps it fragrant. It's patience that gives milk
to the male camel still nursing in its third year,
and patience is what the prophets show to us.

The beauty of careful sewing on a shirt
is the patience it contains.

Friendship and loyalty have patience
as the strength of their connections.

Feeling lonely and ignoble indicates
that you haven't been patient.

Be with those who mix with God
as honey blends with milk, and say,

'Anything that comes and goes,
rises and sets,
is not what I love.'

Live in the one who created the prophets,
else you'll be like a caravan fire left
to flare itself out alone beside the road.

Emptiness

Consider the difference
in our actions and God's actions.

We often ask, 'Why did you do that?'
or 'Why did I act like that?'

We do act, and yet everything we do
is God's creative action.

We look back and analyze the events
of our lives, but there is another way
of seeing, a backward-and-forward-at-once
vision, that is not rationally understandable.

Only God can understand it.
Satan made the excuse, *You caused me to fall,*
whereas Adam said to God, *We did this
to ourselves.* After this repentance,
God asked Adam, *Since all is within
my foreknowledge, why didn't you
defend yourself with that reason?*

Adam answered, *I was afraid,
and I wanted to be reverent.*

Whoever acts with respect will get respect.
Whoever brings sweetness will be served almond cake.
Good women are drawn to be with good men.

Honor your friend.
Or treat him rudely,
and see what happens!

Love, tell an incident now
that will clarify this mystery
of how we act freely, and are yet
compelled. One hand shakes with palsy.
Another shakes because you slapped it away.

Both tremblings come from God,
but you feel guilty for the one,
and what about the other?

These are intellectual questions.
The spirit approaches the matter
differently. Omar once had a friend, a scientist,
Bu'l-Hakam, who was flawless at solving
empirical problems, but he could not follow Omar
into the area of illumination and wonder.

Now I return to the text, 'And He is with you,
wherever you are,' but when have I ever left it!

Ignorance is God's prison.
Knowing is God's palace.

We sleep in God's unconsciousness.
We wake in God's open hand.

We weep God's rain.
We laugh God's lightning.

Fighting and peacefulness
both take place within God.

Who are we then
in this complicated world-tangle,
that is really just the single, straight
line down at the beginning of *ALLAH*?

Nothing.
We are
emptiness.

*   *   *   *

When you are with everyone but me,
                              you're with no one.
When you are with no one but me,
                              you're with everyone.

Instead of being so bound up *with* everyone,
                              be everyone.
When you become that many, you're nothing.
                              Empty.

*   *   *   *

No Flag

I used to want buyers for my words.
Now I wish someone would buy me away from words.

I've made a lot of charmingly profound images,
scenes with Abraham, and Abraham's father, Azar,
who was also famous for icons.

I'm so tired of what I've been doing.

Then one image without form came,
and I quit.

Look for someone else to tend the shop.
I'm out of the image-making business.

Finally I know the freedom
of madness.

A random image arrives. I scream,
'Get out!' It disintegrates.

Only love.
Only the holder the flag fits into,
and wind. No flag.

The Food Sack

One day a sufi sees an empty food sack hanging on a nail.
He begins to turn and tear his shirt, saying,
Food for what needs no food!
A cure for hunger!

His burning grows and others join him,
shouting and moaning in the love-fire.

An idle passerby comments, 'It's only an empty sack.'

The sufi says, *Leave. You want what we do not want.*
You are not a lover.

A lover's food is the love of bread,
not the bread. No one who really loves,
loves existence.

Lovers have nothing to do with existence.
They collect the interest without the capital.

No wings, yet they fly all over the world. No hands,
but they carry the polo ball from the field.

That dervish got a sniff of reality.
Now he weaves baskets of pure vision.

Lovers pitch tents on a field of nowhere.
They are all one color like that field.

A nursing baby does not know the taste of roasted meat.
To a spirit the foodless scent is food.

To an Egyptian, the Nile looks bloody.
To an Israelite, clear.
What is a highway to one is disaster to the other.

The Night Air

A man on his deathbed left instructions
for dividing up his goods among his three sons.
He had devoted his entire spirit to those sons.
They stood like cypress trees around him,
quiet and strong,
                        He told the town judge,
'Whichever of my sons is *laziest*,
give him *all* the inheritance.'

Then he died, and the judge turned to the three,
'Each of you must give some account of your laziness,
so I can understand just *how* you are lazy.'

Mystics are experts in laziness. They rely on it,
because they continuously see God working all around them.
The harvest keeps coming in, yet they
never even did the plowing!

'Come on. Say something about the ways you are lazy.'

Every spoken word is a covering for the inner self.
A little curtain-flick no wider than a slice
of roast meat can reveal hundreds of exploding suns.
Even if what is being said is trivial and wrong,
the listener hears the source. One breeze comes
from across a garden. Another from across the ash-heap.
Think how different the voices of the fox
and the lion, and what they tell you!

Hearing someone is lifting the lid off the cooking pot.
You learn what's for supper. Though some people
can know just by the smell, a sweet stew
from a sour soup cooked with vinegar.

A man taps a clay pot before he buys it
to know by the sound if it has a crack.

The eldest of the three brothers told the judge,
'I can know a man by his voice,
                              and if he won't speak,
I wait three days, and then I know him intuitively.'

The second brother, 'I know him when he speaks,
and if he won't talk, I strike up a conversation.'

'But what if he knows that trick?' asked the judge.

Which reminds me of the mother who tells her child,
'When you're walking through the graveyard at night
and you see a boogeyman, run *at* it,
and it will go away.'

'But what,' replies the child, 'if the boogeyman's
mother has told it to do the same thing?
Boogeymen have mothers too.'

The second brother had no answer.

The judge then asked the youngest brother,
'What if a man cannot be made to say anything?
How do you learn his hidden nature?'

'I sit in front of him in silence,
and set up a ladder made of patience,
and if in his presence a language from beyond joy
and beyond grief begins to pour from *my* chest,
I know that his soul is as deep and bright
as the star Canopus rising over Yemen.

And so when I start speaking a powerful right arm
of words sweeping down, I know *him* from what I say,
and how I say it, because there's a window open
between us, mixing the night air of our beings.'

The youngest was, obviously,
the laziest. He won.

Only Breath

Not Christian or Jew or Muslim, not Hindu,
Buddhist, sufi, or zen. Not any religion,

or cultural system. I am not from the East
or the West, not out of the ocean or up

from the ground, not natural or ethereal, not
composed of elements at all. I do not exist,

am not an entity in this world or the next,
did not descend from Adam and Eve or any

origin story. My place is placeless, a trace
of the traceless. Neither body or soul,

I belong to the beloved, have seen the two
worlds as one and that one call to and know,

first, last, outer, inner, only that
breath breathing human being.

*   *   *   *

There is a way between voice and presence
where information flows.

In disciplined silence it opens.
With wandering talk it closes.

4. Spring Giddiness:

Stand in the Wake of This Chattering and Grow Airy

ON SPRING GIDDINESS

Springtime — when ecstasy seems the natural way to be and any other out of tune with the season of soul growth. Song, airy silence, a lively conversation between plants. No urgency about what gets said or not said. We feel part of some hilarious nub pulling up through the surface into light or lying back in a wagon going who knows where. The weather of Spring in Persia and Turkey and in the southeastern United States is all one long extravagant absorption with ground and sky, the fragrances and what unfolds from within. In lucky places such as these, Spring is not so much a metaphor for a state of attunement as it *is* that attunement. Or say it this way: for a mystic, the inner world is a weather that contains the universe and uses it as symbolic language.

Spring

Again, the violet bows to the lily.
Again, the rose is tearing off her gown!

The green ones have come from the other world,
tipsy like the breeze up to some new foolishness.

Again, near the top of the mountain
the anemone's sweet features appear.

The hyacinth speaks formally to the jasmine,
'Peace be with you.' 'And peace to you, lad!
Come walk with me in this meadow.'

Again, there are sufis everywhere!

The bud is shy, but the wind removes
her veil suddenly, 'My friend!'

The Friend is here like water in the stream,
like a lotus on the water.

The narcissus winks at the wisteria,
'Whenever you say.'

And the clove to the willow, 'You are the one
I hope for.' The willow replies, 'Consider
these chambers of mine yours. Welcome!'

The apple, 'Orange, why the frown?'
'So that those who mean harm
will not see my beauty.'

The ringdove comes asking, 'Where,
where is the Friend?'

With one note the nightingale
indicates the rose.

Again, the *season* of Spring has come
and a spring-source rises under everything,
a moon sliding from the shadows.

Many things must be left unsaid, because it's late,
but whatever conversation we haven't had
tonight, we'll have tomorrow.

Where Everything Is Music

Don't worry about saving these songs!
And if one of our instruments breaks,
it doesn't matter.

We have fallen into the place
where everything is music.
The strumming and the flute notes
rise into the atmosphere,
and even if the whole world's harp
should burn up, there will still be
hidden instruments playing.

So the candle flickers and goes out.
We have a piece of flint, and a spark.

This singing art is sea foam.
The graceful movements come from a pearl
somewhere on the ocean floor.

Poems reach up like spindrift and the edge
of driftwood along the beach, wanting!

They derive
from a slow and powerful root
that we can't see.

Stop the words now.
Open the window in the center of your chest,
and let the spirits fly in and out.

A Great Wagon

When I see your face, the stones start spinning!
You appear; all studying wanders.
I lose my place.

Water turns pearly.
Fire dies down and doesn't destroy.

In your presence I don't want what I thought
I wanted, those three little hanging lamps.

Inside your face the ancient manuscripts
seem like rusty mirrors.

You breathe; new shapes appear,
and the music of a desire as widespread
as Spring begins to move
like a great wagon.
                Drive slowly.
Some of us walking alongside
are lame!

*   *   *   *

Today, like every other day, we wake up empty
and frightened. Don't open the door to the study
and begin reading. Take down a musical instrument.

Let the beauty we love be what we do.
There are hundreds of ways to kneel and kiss the ground.

*   *   *   *

Out beyond ideas of wrongdoing and rightdoing,
there is a field. I'll meet you there.

When the soul lies down in that grass,
the world is too full to talk about.
Ideas, language, even the phrase *each other*
doesn't make any sense.

*   *   *   *

The breeze at dawn has secrets to tell you.
                    Don't go back to sleep.
You must ask for what you really want.
                    Don't go back to sleep.
People are going back and forth across the doorsill
                    where the two worlds touch.
The door is round and open.
                    Don't go back to sleep.

*   *   *   *

I would love to kiss you.
The price of kissing is your life.

Now my loving is running toward my life shouting,
What a bargain, let's buy it.

*   *   *   *

Daylight, full of small dancing particles
and the one great turning, our souls
are dancing with you, without feet, they dance.
Can you see them when I whisper in your ear?

* * * *

They try to say what you are, spiritual or sexual?
They wonder about Solomon and all his wives.

In the body of the world, they say, there is a soul
and you are that.

But we have ways within each other
that will never be said by anyone.

* * * *

Come to the orchard in Spring.
There is light and wine, and sweethearts
        in the pomegranate flowers.

If you do not come, these do not matter.
If you do come, these do not matter.

Spring Is Christ

Everyone has eaten and fallen asleep. The house is empty.
We walk out to the garden to let the apple meet the peach,
to carry messages between rose and jasmine.

Spring is Christ,
raising martyred plants from their shrouds.

Their mouths open in gratitude, wanting to be kissed.
The glow of the rose and the tulip means a lamp
is inside. A leaf trembles. I tremble

in the wind-beauty like silk from Turkestan.
The censer fans into flame.

This wind is the Holy Spirit.
The trees are Mary.
Watch how husband and wife play subtle games with their hands.
Cloudy pearls from Aden are thrown across the lovers,
as is the marriage custom.

The scent of Joseph's shirt comes to Jacob.
A red carnelian of Yemeni laughter is heard
by Muhammad in Mecca.

We talk about this and that. There's no rest
except on these branching moments.

Shreds of Steam

Light again, and the one who brings light!
Change the way you live!

From the ocean vat, wine fire in each cup!
Two or three of the long dead wake up.
Two or three drunks become lion hunters.

Sunlight washes a dark face.
The flower of what's true opens in the face.
Meadowgrass and garden ground grow damp again.
A strong light like fingers massages our heads.
No dividing these fingers from those.

Draw back the lock bolt.
One level flows into another.
Heat seeps into everything.

The passionate pots boil.
Clothing tears into the air.
Poets fume shreds of steam,
never so happy as out in the light!

The Steambath

Steam fills the bath, and frozen figures on the wall
open their eyes, wet and round, Narcissus eyes
that see enormous distances, and new ears
that love the details of any story. The figures dance
like friends diving and coming up and diving again.

Steam spills into the courtyard. It's the noise
of resurrection! They move from one corner
laughing across to the opposite corner. No one notices
how steam opens the rose of each mind,
fills every beggar's cup solid with coins.
Hold out a basket. It fills up so well
that emptiness becomes what you want.

The judge and the accused forget the sentencing.
Someone stands up to speak, and the wood of the table
becomes holy. The tavern in that second is actually *made*
of wine. The dead drink it in.
                              Then the steam evaporates.
Figures sink back into the wall, eyes blank,
ears just lines.
                Now it's happening again, outside.
The garden fills with bird and leaf sounds.

We stand in the wake of this chattering and grow airy.
How can anyone say what happens, even if each of us
dips a pen a hundred millions times into ink?

The Ground Cries Out

I feel like the ground, astonished
at what the atmosphere has brought to it. What I know
is growing inside me. Rain makes
every molecule pregnant with a mystery.
We groan with women in labor.
The ground cries out, *I Am Truth* and *Glory Is Here*,
breaks open, and a camel is born out of it.
A branch falls from a tree, and there's a snake.

Muhammad said, *A faithful believer is a good camel,*
always looking to its master, who takes perfect care.
He brands the flank.
He sets out hay.
He binds the knees with reasonable rules,
and now he loosens all bindings and lets his camel dance,
tearing the bridle and ripping the blankets.

The field itself sprouts new forms,
while the camel dances over them, imaginary
plants no one has thought of,
but all these new seeds, no matter how they try,
do not reveal the other sun.
They hide it.
Still, the effort is joy,
one by one to keep uncovering
pearls in oyster shells.

Unfold Your Own Myth

Who gets up early to discover the moment light begins?
Who finds us here circling, bewildered, like atoms?
Who comes to a spring thirsty
and sees the moon reflected in it?
Who, like Jacob blind with grief and age,
smells the shirt of his lost son
and can see again?
Who lets a bucket down and brings up
a flowing prophet? Or like Moses goes for fire
and finds what burns inside the sunrise?

Jesus slips into a house to escape enemies,
and opens a door to the other world.
Solomon cuts open a fish, and there's a gold ring.
Omar storms in to kill the prophet
and leaves with blessings.
Chase a deer and end up everywhere!
An oyster opens his mouth to swallow one drop.
Now there's a pearl.

A vagrant wanders empty ruins.
Suddenly he's wealthy.

But don't be satisfied with stories, how things
have gone with others. Unfold
your own myth, without complicated explanation,
so everyone will understand the passage,
We have opened you.

Start walking toward Shams. Your legs will get heavy
and tired. Then comes a moment
of feeling the wings you've grown,
lifting.

Not a Day on Any Calendar

Spring, and everything outside is growing,
even the tall cypress tree.
We must not leave this place.
Around the lip of the cup we share, these words,

> *My Life Is Not Mine.*

If someone were to play music, it would have to be very sweet.
We're drinking wine, but not through lips.
We're sleeping it off, but not in bed.
Rub the cup across your forehead.
This day is outside living and dying.

Give up wanting what other people have.
That way you're safe.
'Where, where can I be safe?' you ask.

This is not a day for asking questions,
not a day on any calendar.
This day is conscious of itself.
This day is a lover, bread, and gentleness,
more manifest than saying can say.

Thoughts take form with words,
but this daylight is beyond and before
thinking and imagining. Those two,
they are so thirsty, but this gives smoothness
to water. Their mouths are dry, and they are tired.

The rest of this poem is too blurry
for them to read.

Flutes for Dancing

It's lucky to hear the flutes for dancing
coming down the road. The ground is glowing.
The table set in the yard.

We will drink all this wine tonight
because it's Spring. It is.
It's a growing sea. We're clouds
over the sea,
or flecks of matter
in the ocean when the ocean seems lit from within.
I know I'm drunk when I start this ocean talk.

Would you like to see the moon split
in half with one throw?

The Shape of My Tongue

This mirror inside me shows . . .
I can't say what, but I can't not know!

I run from body. I run from spirit.
I do not belong anywhere.

I'm not alive!
You smell the decay?

You talk about my craziness.
Listen rather to the honed–blade sanity I say.

This gourd head on top of a dervish robe,
do I look like someone you know?

This dipper gourd full of liquid,
upsidedown and not spilling a drop!

Or if it spills, it drops into God
and rounds into pearls.

I form a cloud over that ocean
and gather spillings.

When Shams is here,
I rain.

After a day or two, lilies sprout,
the shape of my tongue.

The Grasses

The same wind that uproots trees
makes the grasses shine.

The lordly wind loves the weakness
and the lowness of grasses.
Never brag of being strong.

The axe doesn't worry how thick the branches are.
It cuts them to pieces. But not the leaves.
It leaves the leaves alone.

A flame doesn't consider the size of the woodpile.
A butcher doesn't run from a flock of sheep.

What is form in the presence of reality?
Very feeble. Reality keeps the sky turned over
like a cup above us, revolving. Who turns
the sky wheel? The universal intelligence.

And the motion of the body comes
from the spirit like a waterwheel
that's held in a stream.

The inhaling-exhaling is from spirit,
now angry, now peaceful.

Wind destroys, and wind protects.

There is no reality but God,
says the completely surrendered sheikh,
who is an ocean for all beings.

The levels of creation are straws in that ocean.
The movement of the straws comes from an agitation
in the water. When the ocean wants the straws calm,
it sends them close to shore. When it wants them
back in the deep surge, it does with them
as the wind does with the grasses.
                                        This never ends.

The Sheikh Who Played with Children

A certain young man was asking around,
'I need to find a wise person. I have a problem.'

A bystander said, 'There's no one with intelligence
in our town except that man over there
playing with the children,

                     the one riding the stick-horse.

He has keen, fiery insight and vast dignity
like the night sky, but he conceals it
in the madness of child's play.'

The young seeker approached the children, 'Dear father,
you who have become as a child, tell me a secret.'

'Go away. This is not a day
for secrets.'

               'But please! Ride your horse this way,
just for a minute.'

                     The sheikh play-galloped over.
'Speak quickly. I can't hold this one still for long.
Whoops. Don't let him kick you.

                        This is a wild one!'

The young man felt he couldn't ask his serious question
in the crazy atmosphere, so he joked,

                     'I need to get married.
Is there someone suitable on this street?'

'There are three kinds of women in the world.
Two are griefs, and one is a treasure to the soul.
The first, when you marry her, is all yours.
The second is half-yours, and the third
is not yours at all.

               Now get out of here,
before this horse kicks you in the head! Easy now!'

The sheikh rode off among the children.
The young man shouted, 'Tell me more about the kinds of women!'

The sheikh, on his cane horsie, came closer,
'The virgin of your first love is all yours.
She will make you feel happy and free. A childless widow
is the second. She will be half-yours. The third,
who is nothing to you, is a married woman with a child.
By her first husband she had a child, and all her love
goes into that child. She will have no connection with you.
Now watch out.
                    Back away.
                              I'm going to turn this rascal around!'

He gave a loud whoop and rode back,
calling the children around him.

'One more question, Master!'
                              The sheikh circled,
'What is it? Quickly! That rider over there needs me.
I think I'm in love.'
                    'What is this playing that you do?
Why do you hide your intelligence so?'
                                        'The people here
want to put me in charge. They want me to be
judge, magistrate, and interpreter of all the texts.

The knowing I have doesn't want that. It wants to enjoy itself.
I am a plantation of sugarcane, and at the same time
I'm eating the sweetness.'
                              Knowledge that is acquired
is not like this. Those who have it worry if
audiences like it or not.
                              It's a bait for popularity.

Disputational knowing wants customers.
It has no soul.
              Robust and energetic,

before a responsive crowd, it slumps when no one is there.
The only real customer is God.
                              Chew quietly
your sweet sugarcane God–Love, and stay
playfully childish.
                    Your face
will turn rosy with illumination
like the redbud flowers.

*   *   *   *

Let the lover be disgraceful, crazy,
absentminded. Someone sober
will worry about things going badly.
Let the lover be.

*   *   *   *

All day and night, music,
a quiet, bright
reedsong. If it
fades, we fade.

5. Feeling Separation:

Don't Come Near Me

ON SEPARATION

We know separation so well because we've tasted the union. The reed flute makes music because it has already experienced changing mud and rain and light into sugarcane. Longing becomes more poignant if in the distance you can't tell whether your friend is going away or coming back. The pushing away pulls you in.

Sometimes I Forget Completely

Sometimes I forget completely
what companionship is.
Unconscious and insane, I spill sad
energy everywhere. My story
gets told in various ways: a romance,
a dirty joke, a war, a vacancy.

Divide up my forgetfulness to any number,
it will go around.
These dark suggestions that I follow,
are they part of some plan?
Friends, be careful. Don't come near me
out of curiosity, or sympathy.

A Man and a Woman Arguing

One night in the desert
a poor Bedouin woman has this to say
to her husband,
                        'Everyone is happy
and prosperous, except us! We have no bread.
We have no spices. We have no water jug.
We barely have any clothes. No blankets

for the night. We fantasize that the full moon
is a cake. We reach for it! We're an embarrassment
even to the beggars. Everyone avoids us.

Arab men are supposed to be generous warriors,
but look at you, stumbling around! If some guest
were to come to us, we'd steal his rags
when he fell asleep. Who is your guide
that leads you to this? We can't even get
a handful of lentils! Ten years' worth
of nothing, that's what we are!'
                        She went on and on.
'If God is abundant, we must be following
an imposter. Who's leading us? Some fake,
that always says, *Tomorrow, illumination
will bring you treasure, tomorrow.*

As everyone knows, that never comes.
Though I guess, it happens very rarely, sometimes,
that a disciple following an imposter can somehow
surpass the pretender. But still I want to know
what this deprivation says about us.'

The husband replied, finally,
                        'How long will you complain

about money and our prospects for money? The torrent
of our life has mostly gone by. Don't worry about
transient things. Think how the animals live.

The dove on the branch giving thanks.
The glorious singing of the nightingale.
The gnat. The elephant. Every living thing
trusts in God for its nourishment.

These pains that you feel are messengers.
Listen to them. Turn them to sweetness. The night
is almost over. You were young once, and content.
Now you think about money all the time.

You used to *be* that money. You were a healthy vine.
Now you're a rotten fruit. You ought to be growing
sweeter and sweeter, but you've gone bad.
As my wife, you should be equal to me.
Like a pair of boots, if one is too tight,
the pair is of no use.

Like two folding doors, we can't be mismatched.
A lion does not mate with a wolf.'

So this man who was happily poor
scolded his wife until daybreak,
when she responded,
                                        'Don't talk to me
about your high station! Look how you act!
Spiritual arrogance is the ugliest of all things.
It's like a day that's cold and snowy,
and your clothes are wet too!

It's too much to bear!
And don't call me your mate, you fraud!
You scramble after scraps of bone
with the dogs.

You're not as satisfied as you pretend!
You're the snake and the snake charmer
at the same time, but you don't know it.
You're charming a snake for money,
and the snake is charming you.

You talk about God a lot, and you make me feel guilty
by using that word. You better watch out!
That word will poison you, if you use it
to have power over me.'

So the rough volume of her talking
fell on the husband, and he fought back,

                                        'Woman,
this poverty is my deepest joy.
This bare way of life is honest and beautiful.
We can hide nothing when we're like this.
You say I'm really arrogant and greedy,
and you say I'm a snake charmer and a snake,
but those nicknames are for you.

In your anger and your wantings
you see those qualities in me.
I want nothing from this world.

You're like a child that has turned round and round,
and now you think the house is turning.

It's your eyes that see wrong. Be patient,
and you'll see the blessings and the lord's light

in how we live.'
                    This argument continued
throughout the day, and even longer.

*   *   *   *

A night full of talking that hurts,
my worst held-back secrets. Everything
has to do with loving and not loving.
This night will pass.
Then we have work to do.

*   *   *   *

An Empty Garlic

You miss the garden,
because you want a small fig from a random tree.
You don't meet the beautiful woman.
You're joking with an old crone.
It makes me want to cry how she detains you,
stinking mouthed, with a hundred talons,
putting her head over the roof edge to call down,
tasteless fig, fold over fold, empty
as dry-rotten garlic.

She has you tight by the belt,
even though there's no flower and no milk
inside her body.
Death will open your eyes
to what her face is: leather spine
of a black lizard. No more advice.

Let yourself be silently drawn
by the stronger pull of what you really love.

The Diver's Clothes Lying Empty

You're sitting here with us, but you're also out walking
in a field at dawn. You are yourself
the animal we hunt when you come with us on the hunt.
You're in your body like a plant is solid in the ground,
yet you're wind. You're the diver's clothes
lying empty on the beach. You're the fish.

In the ocean are many bright strands
and many dark strands like veins that are seen
when a wing is lifted up.
Your hidden self is blood in those, those veins
that are lute strings that make ocean music,
not the sad edge of surf, but the sound of no shore.

Red Shirt

Has anyone seen the boy who used to come here?
Round-faced troublemaker, quick to find a joke, slow
to be serious. Red shirt,
perfect coordination, sly,
strong muscles, with things always in his pocket: reed flute,
ivory pick, polished and ready for his talent.
You know that one.

Have you heard stories about him?
Pharaoh and the whole Egyptian world

collapsed for such a Joseph.
I'd gladly spend years getting word
of him, even third or fourth-hand.

My Worst Habit

My worst habit is I get so tired of winter
I become a torture to those I'm with.

If you're not here, nothing grows.
I lack clarity. My words
tangle and knot up.

How to cure bad water? Send it back to the river.
How to cure bad habits? Send me back to you.

When water gets caught in habitual whirlpools,
dig a way out through the bottom
to the ocean. There is a secret medicine
given only to those who hurt so hard
they can't hope.

The hopers would feel slighted if they knew.

Look as long as you can at the friend you love,
no matter whether that friend is moving away from you
or coming back toward you.

*   *   *   *

Don't let your throat tighten
with fear. Take sips of breath
all day and night, before death
closes your mouth.

* * * *

Dissolver of Sugar

Dissolver of sugar, dissolve me,
if this is the time.
Do it gently with a touch of a hand, or a look.
Every morning I wait at dawn. That's when
it's happened before. Or do it suddenly
like an execution. How else
can I get ready for death?

You breathe without a body like a spark.
You grieve, and I begin to feel lighter.
You keep me away with your arm,
but the keeping away is pulling me in.

* * * *

Pale sunlight,
pale the wall.

Love moves away.
The light changes.

I need more grace
than I thought.

6. Controlling the Desire-Body:

How Did You Kill Your Rooster, Husam?

ON THE DESIRE-BODY

Sufis call the wantings *nafs*. From the urgent way lovers want each other to the sannyasin's search for truth, all moving is from the mover. Every pull draws us to the ocean. Rumi says it's important to live the wantings as they come and not get stuck somewhere, stagnant. He was asked once what to do about a young man caught doing some indecent act. The story doesn't mention what exactly – masturbation, peeping-tomming, whatever wild wantings young men think to do. Rumi told them not to worry about it. 'It just means he's growing his feathers. The dangerous case is a kid who *doesn't* do indecent acts, who then leaves the nest without feathers. One flap and the cat has him.' Be careful, Rumi suggests, about shaming sexual behaviour in an adolescent or anyone who hasn't yet had his or her fill of erotic trancing. Often, the closest we come to surrender is orgasm. In Rumi's symbology the rooster is a symbol for that energy.

So how did Husam kill his rooster? By dissolving into the play. The *nafs* are the energies that keep us moving, stopping nowhere. Union with the divine continually unfolds. Next to the glowing drive-in movie, the junkyard's rusted stacks of old desire-bodies. Let the beauty we love keep turning into action, transmuting to another, another. What have I ever lost by dying? Rumi asks, exchanging one set of *nafs* for the next. Chopped rooster energy becomes another dining room story. Particles of praise shine in the sunlight. Anything you grab hold of on the bank breaks with the river's pressure. When you do things from your soul, the river itself moves through you. Freshness and a deep joy are signs of the current.

Sexual Urgency, What a Woman's Laughter Can Do, and the Nature of True Virility

Someone offhand to the Caliph of Egypt,
'The King of Mosul
has a concubine like no other,
more beautiful than I can describe.
She looks like *this*.'
He draws her likeness on paper.

The Caliph drops his cup.
Immediately he sends his captain to Mosul
with an army of thousands. The siege goes on for a week,
with many casualties, the walls and the towers unsteady,
as soft as wax. The King of Mosul sends an envoy.
'Why this killing? If you want the city,
I will leave and you can have it!
If you want more wealth, that's even easier.'

The captain takes out the piece of paper
with the girl's picture on it. This.
The strong King of Mosul is quick to reply.
'Lead her out. The idol belongs with the idolater.'

When the captain sees her, he falls in love
like the Caliph. Don't laugh at this.
This loving is also part of infinite love,
without which the world does not evolve.
Objects move from inorganic to vegetation
to selves endowed with spirit through the urgency
of every love that wants to come to perfection.

This captain thinks the soil looks fertile,
so he sows his seed. Sleeping, he sees the girl
in a dream. He makes love to her image,
and his semen spurts out.

After a while he begins to wake.
Slowly he senses the girl is not there.
'I have given my seed into nothing.
I shall put this tricky woman to a test.'

A leader who is not captain of his body is not one
to be honored, with his semen spilled so in the sand.
Now he loses all control. He doesn't care
about the Caliph, or about dying.
'I am in love,' he says.

Do not act in such heat.
Take counsel with a master.
But the captain couldn't.

His infatuation is a blackwater wave carrying him away.
Something that doesn't exist makes a phantom
appear in the darkness of a well,
and the phantom itself becomes strong enough
to throw actual lions into the hole.

More advice: it is dangerous to let other men
have intimate connections with the women in your care.
Cotton and fire sparks, those are, together.
Difficult, almost impossible, to quench.

The captain does not return straight to the Caliph,
but instead camps in a secluded meadow.
Blazing, he can't tell ground from sky.
His reason is lost in a drumming sound,

worthless radish and son of a radish.
The Caliph himself a gnat, nothing.

But just as this cultivator tears off the woman's pants
and lies down between her legs, his penis moving
straight to the mark, there's a great tumult
and a rising cry of soldiers outside the tent.
He leaps up with his bare bottom shining
and runs out, scimitar in hand.

A black lion from a nearby swamp
has gotten in among the horses. Chaos.
The lion jumping twenty feet in the air,
tents billowing like an ocean.

The captain quickly approaches the lion,
splits his head with one blow,
and now he's running back to the woman's tent.
When he stretches out her beauty again,
his penis goes even more erect.

The engagement, the coming together, is as with the lion.
His penis stays erect all through it,
and it does not scatter semen feebly.
The beautiful one is amazed at his virility.
Immediately, with great energy she joins with his energy,
and their two spirits go out from them as one.

Whenever two are linked this way, there comes another
from the unseen world. It may be through birth,
if nothing prevents conception,
but a third does come, when two unite in love,
or in hate. The intense qualities born
of such joining appear in the spiritual world.

You will recognize them when you go there.
Your associations bear progeny.
Be careful, therefore. Wait, and be conscious,
before you go to meet anyone.
Remember there are children to consider!

Children you must live with and tend to,
born of your emotions with another, entities
with a form, and speech, and a place to live.
They are crying to you even now.
You have forgotten us. Come back.
Be aware of this. A man and a woman together
always have a spiritual result.

The captain was not so aware. He fell,
and stuck like a gnat in a pot of buttermilk,
totally absorbed in his love affair. Then,
just as suddenly, he's uninterested. He tells
the woman, 'Don't say a word of this to the Caliph.'

He takes her there, and the Caliph is smitten.
She's a hundred times more beautiful than he's imagined.

A certain man asks an eloquent teacher,
'What is true and what false?' 'This is false:
a bat hides from the sun, not from the idea of the sun.

It's the idea that puts fear in the bat and leads it
deeper into the cave. You have an idea
of an enemy that attaches you to certain companions.

Moses, the inner light of revelation,
lit up the top of Sinai, but the mountain
could not hold that light.

Don't deceive yourself that way!
Having the idea is not living
the reality, of anything.

There's no courage in the idea of battle.
The bathhouse wall is covered with pictures
and much talk of heroism. Try to make an idea move
from ear to eye. Then your woolly ears
become as subtle as fibers of light.

Your whole body becomes a mirror,
all eye and spiritual breathing.
Let your ear lead you to your lover.'

So the Caliph is mightily in love with this girl.
His kingdom vanishes like lightning.
If your loving is numb, know this: when what you own
can vanish, it's only a dream, a vanity, breath
through a mustache. It would have killed you.

There are those that say, 'Nothing lasts.'
They're wrong. Every moment they say,
'If there were some other reality,
I would have seen it. I would know about it.'

Because a child doesn't understand a chain of reasoning,
should adults give up being rational?
If reasonable people don't feel the presence of love
within the universe, that doesn't mean it's not there.

Joseph's brothers did not see Joseph's beauty,
but Jacob never lost sight of it. Moses at first
saw only a wooden staff, but to his other seeing
it was a viper and a cause of panic.

Eyesight is in conflict with inner knowing.
Moses' hand is a hand and a source of light.

These matters are as real as the infinite is real,
but they seem religious fantasies to some,
to those who believe only in the reality
of the sexual organs and the digestive tract.

Don't mention the Friend to those.
To others, sex and hunger are fading images,
and the Friend is more constantly, solidly here.
Let the former go to their church, and we'll go to ours.
Don't talk long to skeptics or to those
who claim to be atheists.

So the Caliph has the idea
of entering the beautiful woman,
and he comes to her to do his wanting.

Memory raises his penis, straining it in thought
toward the pushing down and the lifting up
which make that member grow large with delight.

But as he actually lies down with the woman,
there comes to him a decree from God
to stop these voluptuous doings. A very tiny sound,
like a mouse might make. The penis droops,
and desire slips away.

He thinks that whispering sound is a snake
rising off the straw mat. The girl sees his drooping
and sails into fits of laughing at the marvelous thing.
She remembers the captain killing the lion
with his penis standing straight up.

Long and loud her laughter.
Anything she thinks of only increases it,
like the laughter of those who eat hashish.
Everything is funny.

Every emotion has a source and a key that opens it.
The Caliph is furious. He draws his sword.
'What's so amusing? Tell me everything you're thinking.
Don't hold anything back. At this moment
I'm clairvoyant. If you lie, I'll behead you.
If you tell the truth, I'll give you your freedom.'

He stacks seven Qur'ans on top of each other
and swears to do as he says.
When she finally gets hold of herself,
the girl tells all, in great detail. Of the camp
in the meadow, the killing of the lion,
the captain's return to the tent with his penis
still hard as the horn of a rhino.

And the contrast with the Caliph's own member
sinking down because of one mouse-whisper.
Hidden things always come to light.
Do not sow bad seed. Be sure, they'll come up.
Rain and the sun's heat make them rise into the air.
Spring comes after the fall of the leaves,
which is proof enough of the fact of resurrection.
Secrets come out in Spring, out from earth-lips into leaf.
Worries become wine-headaches.
But where did the wine come from? Think.

A branch of blossoms does not look like seed.
A man does not resemble semen. Jesus came
from Gabriel's breath, but he is not in that form.
The grape doesn't look like the vine.
Loving actions are the seed of something

completely different, a living-place.
No origin is like where it leads to.
We can't know where our pain is from.
We don't know all that we've done.
Perhaps it's best that we don't.
Nevertheless we suffer for it.

The Caliph comes back to his clarity. 'In the pride
of my power I took this woman from another,
so of course, someone came to knock on my door.
Whoever commits adultery is a pimp
for his own wife.

If you cause injury to someone, you draw
that same injury toward yourself. My treachery
made my friend a traitor to me. This repetition
must stop somewhere. Here, in an act of mercy.

I'll send you back to the captain,
saying another of my wives is jealous,
and since the captain was brave enough
to bring you back from Mosul
he shall have you in marriage.'

This is the virility of a prophet.
The Caliph was sexually impotent,
but his manliness was most powerful.

The kernel of true manhood is the ability
to abandon sensual indulgences. The intensity
of the captain's libido is less than a husk
compared to the Caliph's nobility in ending
the cycle of sowing lust and reaping
secrecy and vengefulness.

Tattooing in Qazwin

In Qazwin, they have a custom of tattooing themselves
for good luck, with a blue ink, on the back
of the hand, the shoulder, wherever.

A certain man there goes to his barber
and asks to be given a powerful, heroic, blue lion
on his shoulder blade. 'And do it with flair!
I've got Leo ascending. I want plenty of blue!'

But as soon as the needle starts pricking,
he howls,
                    'What are you doing?'
                                        'The lion.'
'Which limb did you start with?'
                                        'I began with the tail.'
'Well, leave out the tail. That lion's rump
is in a bad place for me. It cuts off my wind.'

The barber continues, and immediately
the man yells out,
                    'Oooooooo! Which part now?'
                                        'The ear.'
'Doc, let's do a lion with no ears this time.'
                                        The barber
shakes his head, and once more the needle,
and once more the wailing,
                    'Where are you now?'
                                        'The belly.'
'I like a lion without a belly.'
                                        The master lion-maker
stands for a long time with his fingers in his teeth.
Finally, he throws the needle down.
                                        'No one has ever

been asked to do such a thing! To create a lion
without a tail or a head or a stomach.
God himself could not do it!'

Brother, stand the pain.
Escape the poison of your impulses.
The sky will bow to your beauty, if you do.
Learn to light the candle. Rise with the sun.
Turn away from the cave of your sleeping.
That way a thorn expands to a rose.
A particular glows with the universal.

What is it to praise?
Make yourself particles.

What is it to know something of God?
Burn inside that presence. Burn up.

Copper melts in the healing elixir.
So melt your self in the mixture
that sustains existence.

You tighten your two hands together,
determined not to give up saying 'I' and 'we.'
This tightening blocks you.

The Center of the Fire

No more wine for me!
I'm past delighting in the thick red
and the clear white.

I'm thirsty for my own blood
as it moves into a field of action.

Draw the keenest blade you have
and strike, until the head circles
about the body.

Make a mountain of skulls like that.
Split me apart.

Don't stop at the mouth!
Don't listen to anything I say.
I must enter the center of the fire.

Fire is my child
but I must be consumed
and become fire.

Why is there crackling and smoke?
Because the firewood and the flames
are still talking:

'You are too dense. Go away!'
'You are too wavering. I have solid form.'

In the blackness those two friends keep arguing.
Like a wanderer with no face.
Like the most powerful bird in existence
sitting on its perch, refusing to move.

What can I say to someone so curled up with wanting,
so constricted in his love?

Break your pitcher against a rock.
We don't need any longer
to haul pieces of the ocean around.

We must drown, away from heroism,
and descriptions of heroism.

Like a pure spirit lying down, pulling
its body over it, like a bride her husband
for a cover to keep her warm.

*   *   *   *

Someone who goes with half a load of bread
to a small place that fits like a nest around him,
someone who wants no more, who's not himself
longed for by anyone else,

he is a letter to everyone. You open it.
It says, *Live*.

*   *   *   *

The mystery does not get clearer by repeating the question,
nor is it bought with going to amazing places.

Until you've kept your eyes
and your wanting still for fifty years,
you don't begin to cross over from confusion.

Muhammad and the Huge Eater

Husam demands that we begin Book V.
Ziya-Haqq, the radiance of truth,

                                        Husamuddin,
master to the pure masters,
if my human throat were not so narrow,
I would praise you as you should be praised,
in some language other than this word-language,

but a domestic fowl is not a falcon.
We must mix the varnish we have
and brush it on.

I'm not talking to materialists. When I mention Husam,
I speak only to those who know spiritual secrets.
Praise is simply drawing back the curtains
to let his qualities in.
                        The sun,
of course, remains apart
from what I say.

What the sayer of praise is really praising is
himself, by saying implicitly,
'My eyes are clear.'

Likewise, someone who criticizes is criticizing
himself, saying implicitly, 'I can't see very well
with my eyes so inflamed.'

Don't ever feel sorry for someone
who wants to be the sun, that other sun,
the one that makes rotten things fresh.

And don't ever envy someone
who wants to be this world.

Husam is the sun I mean.
He can't be understood with the mind, or said,
but we'll stumble and stagger trying to.
Just because you can't drink all that falls
doesn't mean you give up taking sips
of rainwater. If the nut
of the mystery can't be held,
at least let me touch the shell.

Husam, refresh my words, your words.
My words are only a husk to your knowing,
an earth atmosphere to your enormous spaces.

What I say is meant only to point to that, to you,
so that whoever ever hears these words will not grieve
that they never had a chance to look.

Your presence draws me out from vanity
and imagination and opinion.

Awe is the salve
that will heal our eyes.

And keen, constant listening.
Stay out in the open like a date palm
lifting its arms. Don't bore mouse holes
in the ground, arguing inside some
doctrinal labyrinth.

That intellectual warp and woof keeps you wrapped
in blindness. And four other characteristics
keep you from loving. The Qur'an calls them
four birds. Say *Bismillah*, 'In the name of God,'
and chop the heads off those mischief-birds.

The rooster of lust, the peacock of wanting
to be famous, the crow of ownership, and the duck
of urgency, kill them and revive them
in another form, changed and harmless.

There is a duck inside you.
Her bill is never still, searching through dry
and wet alike, like the robber in an empty house
cramming objects in his sack, pearls, chickpeas,

anything. Always thinking, 'There's no time!
I won't get another chance!'

A True Person is more calm and deliberate.
He or she doesn't worry about interruptions.

But that duck is so afraid of missing out
that it's lost all generosity, and frighteningly expanded
its capacity to take in food.

A large group of unbelievers
once came to see Muhammad,
knowing he would feed them.

Muhammad told his friends,
'Divide these guests among you and tend to them.
Since you are all filled with me,
it will be as though I am the host.'

Each friend of Muhammad chose a guest,
but there was one huge person left behind.
He sat in the entrance of the mosque
like thick dregs in a cup.

So Muhammad invited the man to his own household,
where the enormous son of the Ghuzz Turk ate everything,
the milk of seven goats and enough food
for eighteen people!

The others in the house were furious.
When the man went to bed, the maid slammed the door
behind him and chained it shut, out of meanness
and resentment. Around midnight, the man
felt several strong urges at once.

But the door! He works it,
puts a blade through the crack. Nothing.
The urgency increases. The room contracts.
He falls back into a confused sleep and dreams
of a desolate place, since he himself is
such a desolate place.

So, dreaming he's by himself,
he squeezes out a huge amount,
and another huge amount.

But he soon becomes conscious enough
to know that the covers he gathers around him
are full of shit. He shakes with spasms of the shame
that usually keeps men from doing such things.

He thinks, 'My sleep is worse than my being awake.
The waking is just full of food.
My sleep is all *this*.'

Now he's crying, bitterly embarrassed,
waiting for dawn and the noise of the door opening,
hoping that somehow he can get out
without anyone seeing him as he is.

I'll shorten it. The door opens. He's saved.
Muhammad comes at dawn. He opens the door
and becomes invisible so the man won't feel ashamed,
so he can escape and wash himself
and not have to face the door-opener.

Someone completely absorbed in Allah like Muhammad
can do this. Muhammad had seen all that went on
in the night, but he held back from letting the man out,
until all happened as it needed to happen.

Many actions which seem cruel
are from a deep friendship.
Many demolitions are actually renovations.

Later, a meddlesome servant
brought Muhammad the bedclothes.
'Look what your guest has done!'

Muhammad smiles, himself a mercy given to all beings,
'Bring me a bucket of water.'

Everyone jumps up, 'No! Let us do this.
We live to serve you, and this is the kind of hand-work
we can do. Yours is the inner heart-work.'

'I know that, but this is an extraordinary occasion.'

A voice inside him is saying, 'There is great wisdom
in washing these bedclothes. Wash them.'

Meanwhile, the man who soiled the covers and fled
is returning to Muhammad's house. He has left behind
an amulet that he always carried.

He enters and sees the hands of God
washing his incredibly dirty linen.

He forgets the amulet. A great love suddenly enters him.
He tears his shirt open. He strikes his head
against the wall and the door. Blood
pours from his nose.

People come from other parts of the house.
He's shrieking, 'Stay away!'
He hits his head, 'I have no understanding!'
He prostrates himself before Muhammad.

'You are the whole. I am a despicable, tiny,
meaningless piece. I can't look at you.'
He's quiet and quivering with remorse.

Muhammad bends over and holds him and caresses him
and opens his inner knowing.

The cloud weeps, and then the garden sprouts.
The baby cries, and the mother's milk flows.
The nurse of creation has said, *Let them cry a lot.*

This rain-weeping and sun-burning twine together
to make us grow. Keep your intelligence white-hot
and your grief glistening, so your life will stay fresh.
Cry easily like a little child.

Let body needs dwindle and soul decisions increase.
Diminish what you give your physical self.
Your spiritual eye will begin to open.

When the body empties and stays empty,
God fills it with musk and mother-of-pearl.
That way a man gives his dung and gets purity.

Listen to the prophets, not to some adolescent boy.
The foundation and the walls of the spiritual life
are made of self-denials and disciplines.

Stay with friends who support you in these.
Talk with them about sacred texts,
and how you're doing, and how they're doing,
and keep your practices together.

Fasting

There's hidden sweetness in the stomach's emptiness.
We are lutes, no more, no less. If the soundbox
is stuffed full of anything, no music.
If the brain and the belly are burning clean
with fasting, every moment a new song comes out of the fire.
The fog clears, and new energy makes you
run up the steps in front of you.
Be emptier and cry like reed instruments cry.
Emptier, write secrets with the reed pen.
When you're full of food and drink, an ugly metal
statue sits where your spirit should. When you fast,
good habits gather like friends who want to help.
Fasting is Solomon's ring. Don't give it
to some illusion and lose your power,
but even if you have, if you've lost all will and control,
they come back when you fast, like soldiers appearing
out of the ground, pennants flying above them.
A table descends to your tents,
Jesus' table.
Expect to see it, when you fast, this table
spread with other food, better than the broth of cabbages.

Bismillah

It's a habit of yours to walk slowly.
You hold a grudge for years.
With such heaviness, how can you be modest?
With such attachments, do you expect to arrive anywhere?

Be wide as the air to learn a secret.
Right now you're equal portions clay
and water, thick mud.

Abraham learned how the sun and moon and the stars all set.
He said, *No longer will I try to assign partners for God.*

You are so weak. Give up to grace.
The ocean takes care of each wave
till it gets to shore.
You need more help than you know.
You're trying to live your life in open scaffolding.
Say Bismillah, *In the name of God,*
as the priest does with a knife when he offers an animal.

Bismillah your old self
to find your real name.

Wean Yourself

Little by little, wean yourself.
This is the gist of what I have to say.

From an embryo, whose nourishment comes in the blood,
move to an infant drinking milk,
to a child on solid food,
to a searcher after wisdom,
to a hunter of more invisible game.

Think how it is to have a conversation with an embryo.
You might say, 'The world outside is vast and intricate.
There are wheatfields and mountain passes,
and orchards in bloom.

At night there are millions of galaxies, and in sunlight
the beauty of friends dancing at a wedding.'

You ask the embryo why he, or she, stays cooped up
in the dark with eyes closed.

> Listen to the answer.

There is no 'other world.'
I only know what I've experienced.
You must be hallucinating.

After the Meditation

Now I see something in my listeners
that won't let me continue this way.

The ocean flows back in
and puts up a foam barrier,
and then withdraws.

After a while,
it will come in again.

This audience wants to hear more
about the visiting sufi and his friends
in meditation. But be discerning.

Don't think of this as a normal character
in an ordinary story.

The ecstatic meditation ended.
Dishes of food were brought out.

The sufi remembered his donkey
that had carried him all day.

He called to the servant there, 'Please,
go to the stable and mix the barley generously
with the straw for the animal. Please.'

'Don't worry yourself with such matters.
All things have been attended to.'

'But I want to make sure that you wet the barley first.
He's an old donkey, and his teeth are shaky.'
'Why are you telling me this?
I have given the appropriate orders.'

'But did you remove the saddle gently,
and put salve on the sore he has?'

'I have served thousands of guests
with these difficulties, and all have gone away
satisfied. Here, you are treated as family.
Do not worry. Enjoy yourself.'

'But did you warm his water
just a little, and then add only a bit of straw
to the barley?'
                        'Sir, I'm ashamed for you.'
                                                'And please,
sweep the stall clean of stones and dung,
and scatter a little dry earth in it.'

'For God's sake, sir,
leave my business to *me!*'

'And did you currycomb his back?
He loves that.'

'Sir! I am *personally*
responsible for all these chores!'

The servant turned and left at a brisk pace . . .
to join his friends in the street.

The sufi then lay down to sleep
and had terrible dreams about his donkey,
how it was being torn to pieces by a wolf,
or falling helplessly into a ditch.

And his dreaming was right!
His donkey was being totally neglected, weak and gasping,
without food or water all the night long.
The servant had done nothing he said he would.

There are such vicious and empty flatterers
in your life. Do the careful,
donkey-tending work.

Don't trust that to anyone else.
There are hypocrites who will praise you,
but who do not care about the health
of your heart-donkey.
                         Be concentrated and leonine
in the hunt for what is your true nourishment.
Don't be distracted by blandishment-noises,
of any sort.

The Dog in the Doorway

This is how it is when your animal energies,
the *nafs*, dominate your soul:

You have a piece of fine linen
that you're going to make into a coat
to give to a friend, but someone else uses it
to make a pair of pants. The linen
has no choice in the matter.
It must submit. Or, it's like
someone breaks into your house
and goes to the garden and plants thornbushes.
An ugly humiliation falls over the place.

Or, you've seen a nomad's dog
lying at the tent entrance, with his head
on the threshold and his eyes closed.

Children pull his tail and touch his face,
but he doesn't move. He loves the children's
attention and stays humble within it.

But if a stranger walks by, he'll spring up
ferociously. Now, what if that dog's owner
were not able to control it?

A poor dervish might appear: the dog storms out.
The dervish says, 'I take refuge with God
when the dog of arrogance attacks,'
and the owner has to say, 'So do I!
I'm helpless against this creature
even in my own house!

Just as you can't come close,
I can't go out!'

This is how animal energy becomes monstrous
and ruins your life's freshness and beauty.

Think of taking this dog out to hunt!
You'd be the quarry.

* * * *

The light you give off
did not come from a pelvis.

Your features did not begin in semen.
Don't try to hide inside anger
radiance that cannot be hidden.

* * * *

Tending Two Shops

Don't run around this world
looking for a hole to hide in.

There are wild beasts in *every* cave!
If you live with mice,
the cat claws will find you.

The only real rest comes
when you're alone with God.

Live in the nowhere that you came from,
even though you have an address here.

That's why you see things in two ways.
Sometimes you look at a person
and see a cynical snake.

Someone else sees a joyful lover,
and you're both right!

Everyone is half and half,
like the black and white ox.

Joseph looked ugly to his brothers,
and most handsome to his father.

You have eyes that see from that nowhere,
and eyes that judge distances,
how high and how low.

You own two shops,
and you run back and forth.

Try to close the one that's a fearful trap,
getting always smaller. Checkmate,
this way. Checkmate that.

Keep open the shop
where you're not selling fishhooks anymore.
You are the free-swimming fish.

*   *   *   *

Think that you're gliding out from the face of a cliff
like an eagle. Think you're walking
like a tiger walks by himself in the forest.
You're most handsome when you're after food.

Spend less time with nightingales and peacocks.
One is just a voice, the other just a color.

7. Sohbet:

Meetings on the Riverbank

ON *SOHBET*

Sohbet has no English equivalent. It means something like 'mystical conversation on mystical subjects.' The voices in Rumi's poetry come from many points on the inner–outer spectrum. The outer conversations are contained within quotation marks, and the inner ones are continuous and permeate the entire fabric of his poetry. On the most ordinary level, we all sometimes hear ourselves speaking from, say, some habitual pattern of meanness or acceptable optimism; then at other times we surprise ourselves by coming out with wisdom beyond our usual. There's a modulation between realities. This is similar to what happens with the fluid pronoun in Rumi's poetry. The *you* and *I* are sometimes the lover talking to the beloved, the personal self and a without-form presence within and beyond the senses. Yet sometimes that presence, amazingly, speaks to Rumi through the poetry; voices slide back and forth within the same short poem! Often the poem serves as a slippery doorsill place between the two, 'partly in my self and partly outside,' the voices coming from a between-place. This expanding and contracting of identity is one of the exciting aspects of Rumi's art. Everything is conversation.

Human beings are discourse. That flowing moves through you whether you say anything or not. Everything that happens is filled with pleasure and warmth because of the delight of the discourse that's always going on. DISCOURSE 53

Rumi's poetry mirrors back to us this ocean of woven speech too intricate and dynamic for any grammarian to untangle.

Talking in the Night

In the middle of the night,
I cried out,
            'Who lives in this love
I have?'
        You said, 'I do, but I'm not here
alone. Why are these other images
with me?'
            I said, 'They are reflections of you,
just as the beautiful inhabitants of Chigil
in Turkestan resemble each other.'

You said, 'But who is this other *living*
being?'
        'That is my wounded soul.'
Then I brought that soul
to you as a prisoner.
                'This one is dangerous,'
I said. 'Don't let him off easy.'

You winked and gave me one end
of a delicate thread.
                'Pull it tight,
but don't break it.'
            I reached my hand
to touch you. You struck it down.

'Why are you so harsh with me?'

'For good reason. But certainly not
to keep you away! Whoever enters this place
saying *Here I am* must be slapped.

This is not a pen for sheep.

There are no separating distances here.
This is love's sanctuary.

Saladin is how the soul looks. Rub your eyes,
and look again with love at love.'

Talking Through the Door

You said, 'Who's at the door?'
    I said, 'Your slave.'

You said, 'What do you want?'
    'To see you and bow.'

'How long will you wait?'
    'Until you call.'

'How long will you cook?'
    'Till the Resurrection.'

We talked through the door. I claimed
a great love and that I had given up
what the world gives to be in that love.

You said, 'Such claims require a witness.'
    I said, 'This longing, these tears.'

You said, 'Discredited witnesses.'
    I said, 'Surely not!'

You said, 'Who did you come with?'
    'The majestic imagination you gave me.'

'*Why* did you come?'
    'The musk of your wine was in the air.'

'What is your intention?'
    'Friendship.'

'What do you want from me?'
    'Grace.'

Then you asked, 'Where have you been
most comfortable?'
    'In the palace.'

'What did you see there?'
    'Amazing things.'

'Then why is it so desolate?'
    'Because all that can be taken away in a second.'

'Who can do that?'
    'This clear discernment.'

'Where can you live safely then?'
    'In surrender.'

'What is this giving up?'
    'A peace that saves us.'

'Is there no threat of disaster?'
    'Only what comes in your street,
    inside your love.'

'How do you walk there?'
    'In perfection.'

Now silence. If I told more of this conversation,
those listening would leave themselves.

There would be no door,
no roof or window either!

A Mouse and a Frog

A mouse and a frog meet every morning on the riverbank.
They sit in a nook of the ground and talk.

Each morning, the second they see each other,
they open easily, telling stories, and dreams and secrets,
empty of any fear or suspicious holding back.

To watch and listen to those two
is to understand how, as it's written,
sometimes when two beings come together,
Christ becomes visible.

The mouse starts laughing out a story he hasn't thought of
in five years, and the telling might take five years!
There's no blocking the speechflow-river-running-
all-carrying momentum that true intimacy is.

Bitterness doesn't have a chance
with those two.

The God-messenger, Khidr, touches a roasted fish.
It leaps off the grill back into the water.

Friend sits by Friend, and the tablets appear.
They read the mysteries
off each other's foreheads.

But one day the mouse complains, 'There are times
when I want *sohbet*, and you're out in the water,
jumping around where you can't hear me.

We meet at this appointed time,
but the text says, *Lovers pray constantly*.

Once a day, once a week, five times an hour,
is not enough. Fish like we are
need the ocean around us!'

Do camel bells say, *Let's meet back here Thursday night?*
Ridiculous. They jingle
together continuously,
talking while the camel walks.

Do you pay regular visits to *yourself?*
Don't argue or answer rationally.

Let us die,
            and dying, reply.

The Long String

The mouse asks the beloved frog,
                        'Do you know
what you are to me? During the day,
you're my energy for working. At night,
you're my deepest sleep.
                    But could we be together
outside of time as well as inside?

Physically, we meet only at breakfast.
Your absence during the rest of the day

enters all my cravings!
                    I drink
five hundred times too much.
                              I eat
like a bulimic trying to die.
                              Help me!

I know I'm not worth it,
but your generosity is so vast!

Let your sunlight shine on this piece of dung,
and dry it out, so I can be used for fuel
to warm and light up a bathhouse.

Look on the terrible and stupid things I've done,
and cause herbs and eglantine to grow out of them.

The sun does this with the ground.
Think what glories God can make
from the fertilizer of sinning!'

The mouse continues to beg, 'My friend,
I know I'm ugly to you.
                        I'm ugly to me!
I'm perfectly ugly!
                    But look, you'll be sad
when I die, won't you? You'll sit by my grave
and weep a little?
                   All I'm asking is,
be with me that little bit of time
while I'm still alive!
Now. I want you *NOW!*'

A certain rich man was accustomed to honor a sufi
by giving him pieces of silver.

'Would you like *one* piece of silver now,
O Lord of my Spirit, or *three* at breakfast
tomorrow morning?'
                          The sufi answered,
'I love the half a coin that I have already in my hand
from yesterday more than the promise of a whole one
today, or the promise of a hundred tomorrow.
A sufi is the child of *this* moment.'

Back to the mouse, who says,
                          'The slap of Now
has cash in its hand. Give me slaps,
on the neck, anywhere!'

Soul of my soul of the soul of a hundred universes,
be water in this now-river, so jasmine flowers
will lift on the brim, and someone far off
can notice the flower-colors and know
there's water here.

'The sign is in the face.' You can look at an orchard
and tell if it rained last night. That freshness
is the sign.

Again, the mouse,
                          'Friend, I'm made from the ground,
and for the ground. You're of the water.

I'm always standing on the bank calling to you.
Have mercy. I can't follow you into the water.
Isn't there some way we can be in touch?
A messenger? Some reminder?'

The two friends decided that the answer
was a long, a *longing!* string, with one end tied
to the mouse's foot and the other to the frog's,

so that by pulling on it their secret connection
might be remembered and the two could meet,
as the soul does with the body.

The froglike soul often escapes from the body
and soars in the happy water. Then the mouse body
pulls on the string, and the soul thinks,

                              Damn.
I have to go back on the riverbank and talk
with that scatterbrained mouse!

                    You'll hear more about this
when you really wake up, on Resurrection Day!

So the mouse and the frog tied the string,
even though the frog had a hunch some tangling
was to come.

              Never ignore those intuitions.
When you feel some slight repugnance about doing something,
listen to it. These premonitions come from God.

Remember the story of the military elephant
who would not move toward the Kaaba. Paralyzed
in that direction, yet swift if pointed toward Yemen.
It had some in-knowing from the unseen.

So the prophet Jacob, when his other sons wanted
to take Joseph out in the country for two days,
had a heart-sickness about their going, and it was true,
though divine destiny prevailed, despite his foreboding,
as it will.

            It's not always a blind man
who falls in a pit. Sometimes it's one who can see.

A holy one does sometimes fall,
but by that tribulation, he or she ascends,
escapes many illusions, escapes

conventional religion, escapes
being so bound to phenomena.

Think of how PHENOMENA come trooping
out of the desert of non-existence
into this materiality.
                    Morning and night,
they arrive in a long line and take over
from each other, 'It's my turn now. Get out!'

A son comes of age, and the father packs up.
This place of phenomena is a wide exchange
of highways, with everything going all sorts
of different ways.
                    We seem to be sitting still,
but we're actually moving, and the fantasies
of phenomena are sliding through us
like ideas through curtains.
                    They go to the well
of deep love inside each of us.
They fill their jars there, and they leave.

There is a source they come from,
and a fountain inside here.
                    Be generous.
Be grateful. Confess when you're not.

We can't know
what the divine intelligence
has in mind!

Who am I,
standing in the midst of this
thought-traffic?

The Force of Friendship

A sea cow, a dugong, finds a special pearl
and brings it up on land at night. By the light it gives off
the dugong can graze on hyacinths and lilies.

The excrement of the dugong is precious ambergris
because it eats such beauty. Anyone who feeds on majesty
becomes eloquent. The bee, from mystic inspiration,
fills its rooms with honey.

So the dugong grazes at night in the pearl-glow.
Presently, a merchant comes and drops black loam
over the pearl, then hides behind a tree to watch.

The dugong surges about the meadow like a blind bull.
Twenty times it rushes at nothing, passing the mound
where the pearl is.

           So Satan couldn't see
the spirit center inside Adam.

                 God says, *Descend,*
and a huge pearl from Aden gets buried under dirt.
The merchant knows,

                but the dugong doesn't.

Every clay-pile with a pearl inside
loves to be near any other clay-pile with a pearl,
but those without pearls cannot stand to be near
the hidden companionship.

Remember the mouse on the riverbank?
There's a love-string stretching into the water
hoping for the frog.

               Suddenly a raven grips the mouse
and flies off. The frog too, from the riverbottom,

with one foot tangled in invisible string,
follows, suspended in the air.
                              Amazed faces ask,
'When did a raven ever go underwater
                              and catch a frog?'

The frog answers,
                    This is the force of Friendship.
What draws friends together
does not conform to laws of nature.
Form doesn't know about spiritual closeness.
If a grain of barley approaches a grain of wheat,
an ant must be carrying it. A black ant on black felt.
You can't see it, but if grains go toward each other,
it's there.
              A hand shifts our birdcages around.
Some are brought closer. Some move apart.
Do not try to reason it out. Be conscious
of who draws you and who not.

Gabriel was always there with Jesus, lifting him
above the dark-blue vault, the night-fortress world,
just as the raven of longing carries the flying frog.

The Vigil

Don't go to sleep one night.
What you most want will come to you then.
Warmed by a sun inside, you'll see wonders.

Tonight, don't put your head down.
Be tough, and strength will come.
That which adoration adores
appears at night. Those asleep

may miss it. One night Moses stayed awake
and asked, and saw a light in a tree.

Then he walked at night for ten years,
until finally he saw the whole tree
illuminated. Muhammad rode his horse
through the nightsky. The day is for work.
The night for love. Don't let someone
bewitch you. Some people sleep at night.

But not lovers. They sit in the dark
and talk to God, who told David,
Those who sleep all night every night
and claim to be connected to us, they lie.

Lovers can't sleep when they feel the privacy
of the beloved all around them. Someone
who's thirsty may sleep for a little while,
but he or she will dream of water, a full jar
beside a creek, or the spiritual water you get
from another person. All night, listen
to the conversation. Stay up.
This moment is all there is.

Death will take it away soon enough.
You'll be gone, and this earth will be left
without a sweetheart, nothing but weeds
growing inside thorns.

I'm through. Read the rest of this poem
in the dark tonight.
                           Do I have a head? And feet?

Shams, so loved by Tabrizians, I close my lips.
I wait for you to come and open them.

Two Friends

A certain person came to the Friend's door
and knocked.
              'Who's there?'
'It's me.'

The Friend answered, 'Go away. There's no place
for raw meat at this table.'

The individual went wandering for a year.
Nothing but the fire of separation
can change hypocrisy and ego. The person returned
completely cooked,
walked up and down in front of the Friend's house,
gently knocked.
                'Who is it?'

'You.'

'Please come in, my self,
there's no place in this house for two.
The doubled end of the thread is not what goes through
the eye of the needle.
It's a single-pointed, fined-down, thread end,
not a big ego-beast with baggage.'

But how can a camel be thinned to a thread?
With the shears of practices, with *doing* things.

And with help from the one who brings
impossibilities to pass, who quiets willfulness,
who gives sight to one blind from birth.

Every day that one does something.
Take that as your text.

Every day God sends forth three powerful energies:
One, from the sperm of the father into the mother,
so growth may begin.
Two, a birth from the womb of the ground,
so male and female may spring into existence.
Three, there's a surge up from the surface
into what is beyond dying, that the real beauty
of creating can be recognized.

There's no way to ever say this.

Let's return to the two friends whose thread
became single,
    who spell with their two letters
the original word,

                    BE.

B and *E* tighten around subjects and objects
that one knot may hold them. Two scissor blades
make one cut.
                    And watch two men washing clothes.
One makes dry clothes wet. The other makes
wet clothes dry. They seem to be thwarting each other,
but their work is a perfect harmony.

Every holy person seems to have a different doctrine
and practice, but there's really only one work.

Someone listening to a millstone falls asleep.
No matter. The stone keeps turning.

Water from the mountain
far above the mill keeps flowing down.
The sleepers will get their bread.

Underground it moves, without sound, and without
repetition. Show us where that source of speech is
that has no alphabet. That spaciousness.

Where we are now is a narrow fantasy
that comes from there, and the actual, outside world
is even narrower. Narrowness is pain,
and the cause of narrowness is manyness.

Creation was spoken with one sound, BE.
The two letters, *B* and *E*,
                                        to record it,
came after.
                    The meaning of the sound
and its resonance
                            are one.

There's no way to ever say this,
in so many words! And no place
to stop saying it.

Meanwhile, a lion and a wolf were fighting. . . .

The Servant Who Loved His Prayers

At dawn a certain rich man
wanted to go to the steambaths.
He woke his servant, Sunqur,
                                        'Ho! Get moving! Get the basin

and the towels and the clay for washing
and let's go to the baths.'

Sunqur immediately collected what was needed,
and they set out side by side along the road.

As they passed the mosque, the call to prayer sounded.
Sunqur loved his five-times prayer.

                                        'Please, master,
rest on this bench for a while that I may recite sura 98,
which begins,

                        "You who treat your slave with kindness." '

The master sat on the bench outside while Sunqur went in.
When prayers were over, and the priest and all the worshipers
had left, still Sunqur remained inside. The master waited
and waited. Finally he yelled into the mosque,

                                        'Sunqur,
why don't you come out?'

                                'I can't. This clever one
won't let me. Have a little more patience.
I hear you out there.'

                        Seven times the master waited,
and then shouted. Sunqur's reply was always the same,
'Not yet. He won't let me come out yet.'

                                        'But there's no one
in there but you. Everyone else has left.
Who makes you sit still so long?'

'The one who keeps me in here is the one
who keeps you out there.
The same who will not let you in will not let me out.'

The ocean will not allow its fish out of itself.
Nor does it let land animals in
where the subtle and delicate fish move.

The land creatures lumber along on the ground.
No cleverness can change this. There's only one
opener for the lock of these matters.

Forget your figuring. Forget your self. Listen to your Friend.
When you become totally obedient to that one,
you'll be free.

Imra'u 'l-Qays

Imra'u 'l-Qays, King of the Arabs,
was very handsome, and a poet, full of love songs.

Women loved him desperately.
Everyone loved him, but there came one night
an experience that changed him completely.
He left his kingdom and his family.
He put on dervish robes and wandered
from one weather, one landscape, to another.

Love dissolved his king-self
and led him to Tabuk, where he worked for a time
making bricks. Someone told the King of Tabuk
about Imra'u 'l-Qays, and that king went to visit him
at night.
            'King of the Arabs, handsome Joseph of this age,
ruler of two empires, one composed of territories,
and the other of the beauty of women,
if you would consent to stay with me,
I would be honored. You abandon kingdoms,
because you want more than kingdoms.'

The King of Tabuk went on like this,
praising Imra'u 'l-Qays, and talking theology

and philosophy. Imra'u 'l-Qays kept silent.
Then suddenly he leaned and whispered something
in the second king's ear, and that second, that
second king became a wanderer too.

They walked out of town hand in hand.
No royal belts, no thrones.

This is what love does and continues to do.

It tastes like honey to adults and milk to children.
Love is the last thirty-pound bale.
When you load it on, the boat tips over.

So they wandered around China like birds
pecking at bits of grain. They rarely spoke
because of the dangerous seriousness
of the secret they knew.

That love-secret spoken pleasantly, or in irritation,
severs a hundred thousand heads in one swing.
A love-lion grazes in the soul's pasture,
while the scimitar of this secret approaches.
It's a killing better than any living.

All that world-power wants, really,
is this weakness.

So these kings talked in low tones,
and carefully. Only God knows what they said.

They used unsayable words. Bird language.
But some people have imitated them, learned
a few birdcalls, and gotten prestigious.

All Rivers at Once

Don't unstring the bow.
I am your four-feathered arrow
that has not been used yet.

I am a strong knifeblade word,
not some *if* or *maybe*,
dissolving in air.

I am sunlight slicing the dark.
Who made this night?
A forge deep in the earth-mud.

What is the body?
Endurance.

What is love?
Gratitude.

What is hidden
in our chests?
Laughter.

What else?
Compassion.

Let the beloved be a hat pulled down firmly on my head.
Or drawstrings pulled and tied around my chest.

Someone asks, How does love have hands and feet?
Love is the sprouting bed for hands and feet!

Your father and mother were playing love games.
They came together, and you appeared!

Don't ask what love can make or do!
Look at the colors of the world.

The riverwater moving in all rivers at once.
The truth that lives in Shams' face.

The Blocked Road

I wish I knew what you wanted.
You block the road and won't give me rest.
You pull my lead-rope one way, then the other.
You act cold, my darling!
Do you hear what I say?

Will this night of talking ever end?
Why am I still embarrassed and timid about you?
You are thousands. You are one.
Quiet, but most articulate.

Your name is Spring.
Your name is wine.
Your name is the nausea
that comes from wine!

You are my doubting
and the lightpoints
in my eyes.

You are every image, and yet
I'm homesick for you.

Can I get there?
Where the deer pounces on the lion,
where the one I'm after's
after me?

This drum and these words keep pounding!
Let them both smash through their coverings
into silence.

A Babbling Child

If my words are not saying what you would say,
slap my face. Discipline me as a loving mother does
a babbling child caught up in nonsense.

A thirsty man runs into the sea, and the sea
holds a sword to his throat.

A lily looks at a bank of roses
and wilts and says nothing.

I am a tambourine. Don't put me aside
till the fast dancing starts.
Play me some all along.
Help me with these little sounds.

Joseph is most beautiful when he's completely naked,
but his shirt gives you an idea,
as the body lets you glimpse the glitter
on the water of the soul.

Even if the corpse washer binds my jaw shut,
you'll still hear this song
coming out of my dead-silence.

* * * *

Who sees inside from outside?
Who finds hundreds of mysteries
even where minds are deranged?

See through his eyes what he sees.
Who then is looking out from his eyes?

* * * *

Constant Conversation

Who is luckiest in this whole orchestra? The reed.
Its mouth touches your lips to learn music.
All reeds, sugarcane especially, think only
of this chance. They sway in the canebrakes,
free in the many ways they dance.

Without you the instruments would die.
One sits close beside you. Another takes a long kiss.
The tambourine begs, *Touch my skin so I can be myself.*
Let me feel you enter each limb bone by bone,
that what died last night can be whole today.

Why live some soberer way and feel you ebbing out?
I won't do it.
Either give me enough wine or leave me alone,
now that I know how it is
to be with you in a constant conversation.

Bonfire at Midnight

A shout comes out of my room
where I've been cooped up.
After all my lust and dead living I can still live with you.
You want me to.
You fix and bring me food.
You forget the way I've been.

The ocean moves and surges in the heat
of the middle of the day,
in the heat of this thought I'm having.
Why aren't all human resistances burning up with his thought?

It's a drum and arms waving.
It's a bonfire at midnight on the top edge of the hill,
this meeting again with you.

In Between Stories

Turn from the ocean now
toward dry land.

When you're with children, talk about toys.
From playthings, little by little, they reach
into deeper wisdom and clarity. Gradually,
they lose interest in their toys.

They have a sense of wholeness in them already.
If they were completely demented
they wouldn't play at all.

                      Did you hear that?
It's the man who was looking for treasure.

He wants me to finish his story.
                              You didn't hear him?
Then he must be inside me yelling, 'Over here!
Come over here!'
                         Don't think of him as a seeker, though.
Whatever he's looking for, he is that himself.
How can a lover be anything but the beloved?

Every second he's bowing into a mirror.
If he could see for just a second one molecule
of what's there without fantasizing about it,
he'd explode.
                    His imagination, and he himself,
would vanish, with all his knowledge, obliterated
into a new birth, a perfectly clear view,
a voice that says, *I am God.*

That same voice told the angels to bow to Adam,
because they were identical with Adam.

It's the voice that first said,
There is no Reality but God.
There is only God.
                         Husam pulls me by the ear now,
'Wash your mouth! By trying to say these things,
you conceal them. Just finish telling the story
about the dervish who was looking for treasure.

Your listeners love difficulties, not unity!
Talk about world troubles.
Don't distribute water from the fountain.
They don't want that.
                         In fact, they've loaded themselves
with dirt clods to clog up the fountain.
They'd like to shut it off!'

We are listeners as well as speakers
of this mystery, both of us,
but who else will join
this strange championship?

That's what Husam wants to know!

The Question

One dervish to another, *What was your vision of God's presence?*
I haven't seen anything.
But for the sake of conversation, I'll tell you a story.

God's presence is there in front of me, a fire on the left,
a lovely stream on the right.
One group walks toward the fire, *into* the fire, another
toward the sweet flowing water.
No one knows which are blessed and which not.
Whoever walks into the fire appears suddenly in the stream.
A head goes under on the water surface, that head
pokes out of the fire.
Most people guard against going into the fire,
and so end up in it.
Those who love the water of pleasure and make it their devotion
are cheated with this reversal.
The trickery goes further.
The voice of the fire tells the *truth* saying, *I am not fire.*
I am fountainhead. Come into me and don't mind the sparks.

If you are a friend of God, fire is your water.
You should wish to have a hundred thousand sets of mothwings,
so you could burn them away, one set a night.
The moth sees light and goes into fire. You should see fire

and go toward light. Fire is what of God is world-consuming.
Water, world-protecting.
Somehow each gives the appearance of the other. To these eyes
you have now, what looks like water
burns. What looks like fire
is a great relief to be inside.
You've seen a magician make a bowl of rice
seem a dish full of tiny, live worms.
Before an assembly with one breath he made the floor swarm
with scorpions that weren't there.
How much more amazing God's tricks.
Generation after generation lies down, defeated, they think,
but they're like a woman underneath a man, circling him.
One molecule-mote-second thinking of God's reversal
of comfort and pain is better
than any attending ritual. That splinter
of intelligence is substance.

The fire and water themselves:
accidental, done with mirrors.

The Music

For sixty years I have been forgetful,
every minute, but not for a second
has this flowing toward me stopped or slowed.
I deserve nothing. Today I recognize
that I am the guest the mystics talk about.
I play this living music for my host.
Everything today is for the host.

*   *   *   *

I saw you last night in the gathering,
but could not take you openly in my arms,

so I put my lips next to your cheek,
pretending to talk privately.

*   *   *   *

The Tent

Outside, the freezing desert night.
This other night inside grows warm, kindling.
Let the landscape be covered with thorny crust.
We have a soft garden in here.
The continents blasted,
cities and little towns, everything
become a scorched, blackened ball.

The news we hear is full of grief for that future,
but the real news inside here
is there's no news at all.

*   *   *   *

Friend, our closeness is this:
anywhere you put your foot, feel me
in the firmness under you.

How is it with this love,
I see your world and not you?

*   *   *   *

Listen to presences inside poems,
Let them take you where they will.

Follow those private hints,
and never leave the premises.

8. Being a Lover:

The Sunrise Ruby

ON BEING A LOVER

Being a lover is close to being a worker. When the ruby becomes the sunrise, its transparency changes to a daily discipline. There's a story about a sufi who rips his robe and gives it the name *faraji*, which means 'ripped open' or 'happiness' or 'one who brings the joy of being opened.' It comes from the stem *faraj*, which also refers to the genitals, male and female. The sufi's teacher sees the purity of the name and the action, while others notice only his ragged appearance. Peace and compassion come as coverings are thrown open and the streaming beauty of emotion flows through the lover-worker. Rumi suggests in another poem that being human is a guest house where travelers are welcomed and entertained. The work is to be a good host at the caravanserai.

The Sunrise Ruby

In the early morning hour,
just before dawn, lover and beloved wake
and take a drink of water.

She asks, 'Do you love me or yourself more?
Really, tell the absolute truth.'

He says, 'There's nothing left of *me*.
I'm like a ruby held up to the sunrise.
Is it still a stone, or a world

made of redness? It has no resistance
to sunlight.'

This is how Hallaj said, *I am God*,
and told the truth!

The ruby and the sunrise are one.
Be courageous and discipline yourself.

Completely become hearing and ear,
and wear this sun-ruby as an earring.

Work. Keep digging your well.
Don't think about getting off from work.
Water is there somewhere.

Submit to a daily practice.
Your loyalty to that
is a ring on the door.

Keep knocking, and the joy inside
will eventually open a window
and look out to see who's there.

Water from Your Spring

What was in that candle's light
that opened and consumed me so quickly?

Come back, my friend! The form of our love
is not a created form.

Nothing can help me but that beauty.
There was a dawn I remember

when my soul heard something
from your soul. I drank water

from your spring and felt
the current take me.

You Sweep the Floor

The lord of beauty enters the soul
as a man walks into an orchard
in Spring.
                    Come into me
that way again!
                         Light the lamp
in the eye of Joseph. Cure Jacob's
sadness. Though you never left,
come and sit down here and ask,
'Why are you so confused?'

Like a fresh idea in an artist's mind,
you fashion things before they come into being.

You sweep the floor like the man
who keeps the doorway.
                              When you brush
a form clean, it becomes
what it truly is.

You guard your silence perfectly
like a waterbag that doesn't leak.

You live where Shams lives,
because your heart-donkey was strong enough
to take you there.

Each Note

Advice doesn't help lovers!
They're not the kind of mountain stream
you can build a dam across.

An intellectual doesn't know
what the drunk is feeling!

Don't try to figure
what those lost inside love
will do next!

Someone in charge would give up all his power,
if he caught one whiff of the wine-musk
from the room where the lovers
are doing who-knows-what!

One of them tries to dig a hole through a mountain.
One flees from academic honors.
One laughs at famous mustaches!

Life freezes if it doesn't get a taste
of this almond cake.
                The stars come up spinning
every night, bewildered in love.
                      They'd grow tired
with that revolving, if they weren't.
                          They'd say,
'How long do we have to *do* this!'

God picks up the reed-flute world and blows.
Each note is a need coming through one of us,
a passion, a longing-pain.
                    Remember the lips

where the wind-breath originated,
and let your note be clear.
Don't try to end it.
Be your note.
I'll show you how it's enough.

Go up on the roof at night
in this city of the soul.

Let *everyone* climb on their roofs
and sing their notes!

Sing loud!

Granite and Wineglass

You are granite.
I am an empty wineglass.

You know what happens when we touch!
You laugh like the sun coming up laughs
at a star that disappears into it.

Love opens my chest, and thought
returns to its confines.

Patience and rational considerations leave.
Only passion stays, whimpering and feverish.

Some men fall down in the road like dregs thrown out.
Then, totally reckless, the next morning

they gallop out with new purposes. Love
is the reality, and poetry is the drum

that calls us to that. Don't keep complaining
about loneliness! Let the fear-language of that theme

crack open and float away. Let the priest come down
from his tower, and not go back up!

Buoyancy

Love has taken away my practices
and filled me with poetry.

I tried to keep quietly repeating,
No strength but yours,
but I couldn't.

I had to clap and sing.
I used to be respectable and chaste and stable,
but who can stand in this strong wind
and remember those things?

A mountain keeps an echo deep inside itself.
That's how I hold your voice.

I am scrap wood thrown in your fire,
and quickly reduced to smoke.

I saw you and became empty.
This emptiness, more beautiful than existence,
it obliterates existence, and yet when it comes,
existence thrives and creates more existence!

The sky is blue. The world is a blind man
squatting on the road.

But whoever sees your emptiness
sees beyond blue and beyond the blind man.

A great soul hides like Muhammad, or Jesus,
moving through a crowd in a city
where no one knows him.

To praise is to praise
how one surrenders
to the emptiness.

To praise the sun is to praise your own eyes.
Praise, the ocean. What we say, a little ship.

So the sea-journey goes on, and who knows where!
Just to be held by the ocean is the best luck
we could have. It's a total waking up!

Why should we grieve that we've been sleeping?
It doesn't matter how long we've been unconscious.

We're groggy, but let the guilt go.
Feel the motions of tenderness
around you, the buoyancy.

Music Master

You that love lovers,
this is your home. Welcome!

In the midst of making form, love
made this form that melts form,
with love for the door,
soul the vestibule.

Watch the dust grains moving
in the light near the window.

Their dance is our dance.

We rarely hear the inward music,
but we're all dancing to it nevertheless,

directed by the one who teaches us,
the pure joy of the sun,
our music master.

* * * *

When I am with you, we stay up all night.
When you're not here, I can't go to sleep.

Praise God for these two insomnias!
And the difference between them.

* * * *

The minute I heard my first love story
I started looking for you, not knowing
how blind that was.

Lovers don't finally meet somewhere.
They're in each other all along.

* * * *

We are the mirror as well as the face in it.
We are tasting the taste this minute

of eternity. We are pain
and what cures pain. We are
the sweet cold water and the jar that pours.

*   *   *   *

I want to hold you close like a lute,
so we can cry out with loving.

You would rather throw stones at a mirror?
I am your mirror, and here are the stones.

*   *   *   *

Someone Digging in the Ground

An eye is meant to see things.
The soul is here for its own joy.
A head has one use: for loving a true love.
Legs: to run after.

Love is for vanishing into the sky. The mind,
for learning what men have done and tried to do.
Mysteries are not to be solved. The eye goes blind
when it only wants to see *why*.

A lover is always accused of something.
But when he finds his love, whatever was lost
in the looking comes back completely changed.
On the way to Mecca, many dangers: thieves,
the blowing sand, only camel's milk to drink.
Still each pilgrim kisses the black stone there
with pure longing, feeling in the surface
the taste of the lips he wants.

This talk is like stamping new coins. They pile up,
while the real work is done outside
by someone digging in the ground.

The Phrasing Must Change

Learn about your inner self from those who know such things,
but don't repeat verbatim what they say.
Zuleikha let everything be the name of Joseph, from celery seed
to aloes wood. She loved him so much she concealed his name
in many different phrases, the inner meanings
known only to her. When she said, *The wax is softening
near the fire*, she meant, My love is wanting me.
Or if she said, *Look, the moon is up* or *The willow has new leaves*
or *The branches are trembling* or *The coriander seeds
have caught fire* or *The roses are opening*
or *The king is in a good mood today* or *Isn't that lucky?*
or *The furniture needs dusting* or
The water carrier is here or *It's almost daylight* or
These vegetables are perfect or *The bread needs more salt*
or *The clouds seem to be moving against the wind*
or *My head hurts* or *My headache's better*,
anything she praises, it's Joseph's touch she means,
any complaint, it's his being away.
When she's hungry, it's for him. Thirsty, his name is a sherbet.
Cold, he's a fur. This is what the Friend can do
when one is in such love. Sensual people use the holy names
often, but they don't work for them.
The miracle Jesus did by being the name of God,
Zuleikha felt in the name of *Joseph*.

When one is united to the core of another, to speak of that
is to breathe the name *Hu*, empty of self and filled

with love. As the saying goes, *The pot drips what is in it.*
The saffron spice of connecting, laughter.
The onion smell of separation, crying.
Others have many things and people they love.
This is not the way of Friend and friend.

The Guest House

This being human is a guest house.
Every morning a new arrival.

A joy, a depression, a meanness,
some momentary awareness comes
as an unexpected visitor.

Welcome and entertain them all!
Even if they're a crowd of sorrows,
who violently sweep your house
empty of its furniture,
still, treat each guest honorably.
He may be clearing you out
for some new delight.

The dark thought, the shame, the malice,
meet them at the door laughing,
and invite them in.

Be grateful for whoever comes,
because each has been sent
as a guide from beyond.

Notes

On Rumi

Fariddin Attar (1119–1230) was the great perfumist and physician-poet, author of *The Conference of the Birds*. He is said to have met Rumi in Damascus when Rumi was a boy of twelve traveling with his father. Attar immediately recognized Rumi's spiritual eminence. He saw the father walking ahead of the son and said, 'Here comes a sea followed by an ocean.' He gave the boy his *Asranama*, a book about the entanglement of the soul in the material world.

Annemarie Schimmel has been immersed in Rumi for over forty years. Her scholarship and devotion are magnificent. *The Triumphal Sun: A Study of the Works of Jalaloddin Rumi* (1978) and *I Am Wind, You Are Fire: The Life and Work of Rumi* (1992) are classics in the field.

A Note on the Organization

Alast is the primordial covenant that occurs when God addresses the not-yet-created humanity, 'Am I not your lord? *Alastu bi-rabbikum.*' Rumi hears the question as a creative music that makes all creatures come forth in a loving dance of reply, 'Yes!'

1. The Tavern

On the tavern: Nasruddin is a Middle Eastern trickster figure.

'A Children's Game': Hakim Sanai (d. 1131), the eloquent court poet of Ghazna, was the first to use the *mathnawi* form, rhyming couplets expressing mystical and didactic themes. Rumi borrows many images and phrases and stories from Sanai, particularly from his *Hadiqat al-haqiqa, The Orchard of Truth*. Sanai's earthy style impressed Rumi. His remark that dirty jokes can be instructional finds its way into Book V of the *Mathnawi*, where a number of such jokes are told and explicated. Sanai is also the source of the famous story of the blind man and the elephant, which Rumi changes to a number of people in a darkened room trying to describe an elephant by where they happen to touch it. Sanai got the story from Indian sources. The tricky pun *bargi bi bargi* (the leaves of leaflessness) also comes from Sanai. Rumi uses the image of 'no-leaves' blooming on a winter tree as a beautiful symbol for the state of awareness that has abandoned the world without leaving (!) it.

Hu is the pronoun of divine presence.

'Special Plates': The word *Shams* means 'the sun,' and almost every use of sunlight in Rumi's poetry is a remembrance of Shams of Tabriz, the wandering mystic whom Rumi met in 1244, when he was thirty-seven. Shams was fifty, perhaps sixty. Their Friendship is one of the central icons of mysticism. They merged in a duet of being that became a single note. Teacher and student, lover and beloved, existence and non-existence, light and the source of light, presence and absence, all distinctions dissolved in the mystical conversation (*sohbet*) that they became. Rumi's son, Sultan Velad, writes that Shams passed through all the lower stages of enthusiastic lovers of God and became *qotb-e hama ma shugan*, the pole of the beloved. When he arrived in 1244 in the vicinity of Konya, he was an overwhelming spiritual presence, a wild sunlion, who avoided the society of the learned, especially theologians. He stayed on the outskirts in a caravanserai, home for the homeless and wanderers. One version of the meeting of Rumi and Shams says that their first encounter occurred in the caravanserai of the sugar merchants. Husam Chelebi, Rumi's scribe, was a student of Shams. He also is closely associated with sunlight, 'the radiance of truth, Husamuddin.'

Rumi scholar Annemarie Schimmel provides what facts are known about Shams in her *The Triumphal Sun: A Study of the Works of Jalaloddin Rumi* (London: East-West Publications, 1978), 16–25. Aflaki, a fourteenth-century writer and friend of Rumi's grandson, gives the more legendary version.

2. Bewilderment

'I Have Five Things to Say': Rabia (d. 801), the great woman mystic from Basra, said that God should be loved not out of fear or hope, but for his beauty, and that that beauty is in the heart. She once sat indoors on a lovely Spring day to teach that external magnificence is only a reflection of God's inner kindness and generosity.

The *sema* is the ecstatic dance of turning.

'Saladin's Begging Bowl': Saladin refers to Saladin Zarkub, the goldsmith, the Friend Rumi found after Shams disappeared. There are hagiographic miniatures that show Rumi leading Saladin out of his goldsmith's shop and onto the street to begin the *sema*; Rumi had heard a transcendent music in the goldsmith's hammering. Saladin had come to Konya in 1235, already a student, like Rumi, of Burhan Mahaqqiq. It is said that when Shams arrived, the two (Rumi and Shams) often met in Saladin's shop or in his home. Sometime after Shams's disappearance Saladin became the company that Rumi needed, the reminder of deep presence. Saladin, in a different way from Shams, was also a problem for Rumi's disciples. He was uneducated, almost illiterate. While Shams was a profound student of scripture, Saladin could not recite the first sura of the Qur'an correctly! Rumi, though, recognized him as his next guide.

He that came last year in red [Shams]
appears now in a brown robe [Saladin].

The Friendship was further bonded by the marriage of Rumi's son, Sultan Velad, to Saladin's daughter. Several of Rumi's letters are addressed to the young couple. A number of poems end with Saladin's name in the author's place of honor. In 1258 when Saladin died, Rumi led a glorious mystical dance with flute and drum through the streets of Konya to celebrate the *urs*, the spiritual wedding of a great saint.

'Where Are We?' In Persian the imagery of the last stanza contains a complex pun. *Maku* means 'a weaver's shuttle.' *Ma ku* means 'Where are we?' Rumi often uses elaborate puns that are almost impossible to translate.

3. Emptiness and Silence

'The Reed Flute's Song': The poem is in the *mathnawi* (rhyming couplet) form. One day Husam and Rumi were walking in the gardens of Meram. Husam suggested that Rumi begin a poem in the *mathnawi* form, whereupon Rumi pulled the first eighteen lines of 'The Reed Flute's Song,' which he had already written down, out of his turban. The deep, synchronistic, collaborative coupleting had already begun! Annemarie Schimmel has a beautiful image for what the six books of the *Mathnawi* became during the next twelve years of Rumi and Husam's collaboration. She likens it to a *medrese*, a dervish learning community, and in particular, the Qaratay center in Konya, which was built a few years before the *Mathnawi* was begun. The walls and the ceiling inside are covered with exquisite knotted Kufic script, very complicated so that only the initiated can decipher it. The design as a whole leads the attention upward to a dome, where the inlays change to a star pattern. 'The eye wanders finding no beginning or end,' until it reaches the apex, which is open, and through which at night stars are seen and reflected in a tiny pond in the center of the floor. The ineffable density, woven, rising out of a Qur'anic base, boundaryless yet centered in a starry, small-pond transparency – this is how the *Mathnawi* feels. The Qaratay meeting room, which can still be visited in Konya, makes a fine metaphor. All of Rumi's poetry is discourse with and within a community, *sohbet*, the mystical companionship beyond the limits of time and space.

'Sanai': *Rum* equals *Rome*, a designation for the western half of Anatolia, which was formerly a part of the Roman Empire. This is the source of Rumi's name, 'the one from Roman Anatolia.' In dialectical Arabic to this day, the adjective *rumi* refers to that which is Western or nonindigenous.

'No Flag': Azar was Abraham's father and a famous image maker. In the Qur'an Abraham asks his father, 'Do you take idols for gods?'

4. *Spring Giddiness*

'Unfold Your Own Myth': The line 'Chase a deer and end up everywhere!' is a reference to Ibrahim (d. 783), whose story is given below. A prince of Balkh, Ibrahim represents to the sufis someone who in one visionary moment gives up his external kingdom for the inner majesty. There are striking similarities between his life and Gautama the Buddha's. Balkh seems to have been an area where Buddhism, Islam, and Christianity met and blended; lotus motifs appear on the ancient ruins there. Here is Rumi's account of Ibrahim's epiphany:

Ibrahim, when he was still king, went out hunting. As he galloped after a deer, he became separated from his retinue. His horse was tired and lathered, but still Ibrahim rode. Deep in the wilderness, the fleeing deer turned its head and spoke, 'You were not created for this chase. This deer body did not take shape out of nothingness, so that you might hunt. Supposing you catch me, will that be enough?' Ibrahim heard these words deeply and cried out. He reined in his horse and dismounted. There was a shepherd nearby. 'Take this royal jacket sewn with jewels. Take my horse and my bow. Give me your shepherd's robe of coarse cloth, and tell no one what has happened!' The exchange was made, and Ibrahim set out on his new life. He made such an extraordinary effort to catch the deer and ended up being caught by God! All plans are subject to revision. God lives between a human being and the object of his or her desire. 'It's all a mystical journey to the Friend.' (Discourse #44)

7. Sohbet

'In Between Stories': Husam Chelebi was the scribe to whom Rumi dictated the entire *Mathnawi*, but he was also much more than a secretary. Rumi said that Husam was the source of the words. Rumi claimed only to be the flute. Husam was the flute player and the breath, the *Mathnawi* itself being the song. Husam was a student of Shams. It is through him, then, that the voice of the beloved is made audible. Rumi says that Husam belongs to that class of saints who are not content with silent contemplation but who must express their knowing.

References

The numbers for the quatrains and the odes (# followed by a number) refer to the numbering in Furuzanfar's edition of *Kulliyat-e Shams*, 8 vols. (Teheran: Amir Kabir Press, 1957–1966). The *Mathnawi* references (a roman numeral, I–VI, followed by line numbers) are to Reynold Nicholson's edition (London: Luzac, 1925–1940). The page references to Arberry are to A. J. Arberry's translation, *The Rubaiyat of Jalal al-din Rumi* (London: Emery Walker, 1949).

1. The Tavern

'Who Says Words with My Mouth?' from *Safa Anthology*; 'We have a huge barrel of wine . . . ,' #1319; 'A Community of the Spirit,' #2577; 'There's a strange frenzy in my head . . . ,' #747; 'Drunks fear the police . . . ,' #731; 'A Children's Game,' I, 3426–54; 'Gone, inner and outer . . . ,' #1159; 'The wine we really drink . . . ,' #1301; 'The Many Wines,' IV, 2683–96; 'Special Plates,' #1910; 'Burnt Kabob,' #2738; 'The New Rule,' #1861; 'This that is tormented . . . ,' #190.

2. Bewilderment

'I Have Five Things to Say,' III, 4694–4734; 'Acts of Helplessness,' II, 1680–1708; 'Saladin's Begging Bowl,' #1397; 'Late, by myself . . . ,' #12; 'Does sunset sometimes look . . . ,' #551; 'Be Melting Snow,' #2172; 'The Fragile Vial,' V, 1884–1920, 1959–64; 'Where Are We?' VI, 3288–95, 3306–22; 'The Friend comes into my body . . . ,' #167; 'There is a light seed grain . . . ,' #667; 'Do you think I know . . . ,' #1359.

3. *Emptiness and Silence*

'The Reed Flute's Song,' I, 1–18; 'A Thirsty Fish,' #1823; 'Enough Words?' #2155; 'This World Which Is Made of Our Love for Emptiness,' #950; 'Quietness,' #636; 'Sanai,' #996; 'A Just-Finishing Candle,' V, 672–82; 'Crafts-manship and Emptiness,' VI, 1369–1420; 'Emptiness,' I, 1480–1514; 'When you are with everyone but me . . . ,' #1793; 'No Flag,' #2449; 'The Food Sack,' III, 3014–30; 'The Night Air,' VI, 4876–4916; 'Only Breath,' from a translation quoted in Pir Vilayat Khan's *The Message in Our Time* (New York: Harper & Row, 1978), 426; 'There is a way between voice . . . ,' #337.

4. *Spring Giddiness*

'Spring,' #211; 'Where Everything is Music,' #110; 'A Great Wagon,' #171; 'Today, like every other day . . . ,' #82; 'Out beyond ideas of wrongdoing . . . ,' #158; 'The breeze at dawn . . . ,' #91; 'I would love to kiss you . . . ,' #388; 'Daylight, full of small dancing particles . . . ,' #556; 'They try to say what you are . . . ,' #558; 'Come to the orchard in Spring . . . ,' #914; 'Spring Is Christ,' #2003; 'Shreds of Steam,' #3438; 'The Steambath,' #809; 'The Ground Cries Out,' #3048; 'Unfold Your Own Myth,' #598; 'Not a Day on Any Calendar,' #2728; 'Flutes for Dancing,' #2967; 'The Shape of My Tongue,' #1486; 'The Grasses,' I, 3325–43; 'The Sheikh Who Played with Children,' II, 2338–42, 2384–85, 2400–2430, 2436–38, 2442; 'Let the lover be disgraceful . . . ,' #55; 'All day and night, music . . . ,' #7.

5. *Feeling Separation*

'Sometimes I Forget Completely,' #2537; 'A Man and a Woman Arguing,' I, 2252–2364, 2372–74; 'A night full of talking that hurts . . . ,' #170; 'An Empty Garlic,' #2776; 'The Diver's Clothes Lying Empty,' #2693; 'Red Shirt,' #1924; 'My Worst Habit,' #2779; 'Don't let your throat tighten . . . ,' #825; 'Dissolver of Sugar,' #3019; 'Pale sunlight . . . ,' Arberry, 153b.

6. *Controlling the Desire-Body*

'Sexual Urgency . . . ,' V, 3831–4034; 'Tattooing in Qazwin,' I, 2981–3021; 'The Center of the Fire,' #1304; 'Someone who goes with half a loaf . . . ,' #494; 'The mystery does not get clearer . . . ,' #1088; 'Muhammad and the Huge Eater,' V, 1–149, 163, 167; 'Fasting,' #1739; '*Bismillah*,' #1073; 'Wean Yourself,' III, 49–62; 'After the Meditation,' II, 194–223, 260–63; 'The Dog in the Doorway,' V, 2922–28, 2940–43, 2956–62; 'The light you give off . . . ,' #2; 'Tending Two Shops,' II, 590–93, 602–13; 'Think that you're gliding out . . . ,' #1078.

7. Sohbet

'Talking in the Night,' #1335; 'Talking Through the Door,' #436; 'A Mouse and a Frog,' VI, 2632, 2665–69, 2681–84; 'The Long String,' VI, 2686–2786; 'The Force of Friendship,' VI, 2922–73; 'The Vigil,' #258; 'Two Friends,' I, 3065–3101; 'The Servant Who Loved His Prayers,' III, 3055–76; 'Imra'u 'l-Qays,' VI, 3986–4010; 'All Rivers at Once,' #1126; 'The Blocked Road,' #1837; 'A Babbling Child,' #2083; 'Who sees inside from outside? . . . ,' #497; 'Constant Conversation,' end of #7; 'Bonfire at Midnight,' #2110; 'In Between Stories,' VI, 2252–77; 'The Question,' V, 420–55; 'The Music,' I, 2084–85; 'I saw you last night in the gathering . . . ,' #1035; 'The Tent,' #1051; 'Friend, our closeness is this . . . ,' #25; 'Listen to presences . . . ,' #730.

8. *Being a Lover*

'The Sunrise Ruby,' V, 2020–49; 'Water from Your Spring,' #1001; 'You Sweep the Floor,' #3050; 'Each Note,' #532; 'Granite and Wineglass,' #2357; 'Buoyancy,' #940; 'Music Master,' #1195; 'When I am with you . . . ,' #36; 'The minute I heard my first love story . . . ,' #1246; 'We are the mirror as well as the face . . . ,' #1652; 'I want to hold you close . . . ,' #1080; 'Someone Digging in the Ground,' #617; 'The Phrasing Must Change,' I, 4020–43; 'The Guest House,' V, 3644–46, 3676–80, 3693–95.

Index of Titles

Index of First Lines